101 Mutual Fund FAQs
Frequently Asked Questions
Straight Answers that
Help You Make Good
Investment Decisions

Dian Vujovich

**CHANDLER
HOUSE
PRESS**

Chandler House Press
Worcester, Massachusetts
1999

101 Mutual Fund FAQs:
Straight Answers that Help You Make Good Investment Decisions
Copyright © 1999 by Dian Vujovich

ISBN: 1-886284-23-7
Library of Congress Catalog Card Number 98-74423
First Edition
ABCDEFGHIJK

Published by
Chandler House Press
335 Chandler Street
Worcester, MA 01602 USA

President
Lawrence J. Abramoff

Publisher/Editor-in-Chief
Richard J. Staron

Editorial/Production Manager
Jennifer J. Goguen

Book Design and Production
CWL Publishing Enterprises
3010 Irvington Way
Madison, WI 53713 USA
www.execpc.com/cwlpubent

Chandler House Press books are available at special discounts for bulk purchases. For more information about how to arrange such purchases, please contact Chandler House Press, 335 Chandler Street, Worcester, MA 01602, or call (800) 642-6657, or fax (508) 756-9425, or find us on the World Wide Web at www.tatnuck.com.

Chandler House Press books are distributed to the trade by
National Book Network
4720 Boston Way
Lanham, MD 20706
(800) 462-6420

Disclaimer The opinions expressed herein are solely those of the author and are based on the author's personal experiences. They are not intended to be the norm for all investors. Reasonable care has been taken in the preparation of the text to ensure its clarity and accuracy. This book is sold with the understanding that the author and the publisher are not engaged in rendering legal or accounting services. Laws vary from state to state, and readers with specific financial questions should seek the services of a professional advisor. The author and publisher specifically disclaim any liability, loss, or risk, personal or otherwise, which is incurred as a consequence, directly or indirectly, of the use and application of any of the contents of this book.

Dedication

This book is dedicated to common sense.
When investing in mutual funds, part of that common
sense means understanding that all markets are fickle,
paper profits and losses can't be banked on, and big fat
nest eggs take time to build.

Contents

Foreword

In baseball parlance, *101 Mutual Fund FAQs* is a triple that can be stretched to a "four bagger." Each base relies on a different strength.

For the reader to get to first base, she or he needs to recognize that Dian Vujovich is a very different and insightful mutual funds columnist and author. Dian brings to this subject not only reportorial skills, but she comes from a background of working with investors to solve their mutual fund problems. In other words, "she sold them."

To get to second base, you need to use this work as a reference book. Unlike many other books on mutual funds that are essentially a single paragraph stretched over 200 pages of repetition, this work focuses on 101 frequently asked questions. These FAQs are arrayed in a logical format and broken down into sensible items. Unlike many books which, after they have been read, gather dust, this book can be used by mutual fund investors at each contemplated change in their portfolio of funds.

The triple is reached in the last paragraph of the book, where Dian focuses on the fact that investing in mutual funds should be an ongoing education and talks about how experience can make you a better investor. Both points I heartily agree with. Her final two words are very significant. They are "good luck," which recognizes the random nature of surprise both in the marketplace as well as in the reader's life.

You can come all the way around to home plate with this book if you refer to it as you increase the amount of time and, I hope, pleasure, you spend in studying and successfully investing in mutual funds. Over time, this can translate to you, and perhaps more importantly, to your heirs as a home run.

Now it's your turn at bat, and good luck.

A. Michael Lipper
Chairman of Lipper Analytical Services

Preface

Once I new I was going to write a Q&A book about mutual funds, I asked a travel writer friend of mine if she had any questions about them—figuring, of course, that she'd come up with some dandies. Well, I figured wrong. Instead of saying "Oh yeah, I've always wondered blah blah blah about mutual funds," she looked at me with one of those deer's-eyes-caught-in-the-headlights looks and said, "You know, I don't even know what a mutual fund is, let alone have any questions to ask you about them."

In spite of the fact that mutual funds have become wildly popular investment vehicles over the past ten years, have assets in them currently totaling more than are in bank deposits, and have become one of the favorite product choices for those building personal portfolios and investing in qualified retirement accounts like IRA and 401(k) plans, there is an awful lot people don't know—or understand—about these pooled investments. And it's for all of these people that this book was written.

101 Mutual Fund FAQs is a book that's not only easy-to-read—thanks to its Q&A format—but is chock-full of useful information that the new, the wannabe, the curious, and the savvy fund investor can learn from. Don't think for an instant that this book might be too simple or sophisticated for you. It won't be. This is a for-everyone book with questions in it ranging from basic, simple common sense ones such as "What is a mutual fund?" and "How can they make me any money?" to the more complicated ones like understanding what asset allocation is. Or, why diversification is important, what international fund investing can do for you, how to open an account for your children or grand kids, or, how to have the income checks from your fund sent to you while you vacation in Barbados for the winter months.

The questions used in the *101 Mutual Fund FAQs* came

from a variety of sources including those my friends have asked, ones readers of my nationally syndicated mutual fund's column have asked, those sent to me at my e-mail address (mismutual@aol.com), as well as from conversations I've had with people met at conferences, parties, or sitting next to on planes, boats, and trains. And, while I've collected literally hundreds upon hundreds of questions, the ones selected for this book where chosen with a purpose in mind: to provide you with a well-rounded knowledge of mutual funds along with vital information that can help when you need to make some sound mutual fund investment decisions.

Before reading through this book, keep in mind that mutual funds are an investment product that make sense for some people and don't fit the bill for others. Plus, the returns investors get from the funds they've selected are as varied as the thousands of funds on the marketplace are. And as with all investments, choosing to place your money in a mutual fund means deciding to take on some level of investment risk with your investment capital. All of which means, there are no risk-free investments nor will you be guaranteed any specific returns from your fund investments.

Knowing these few points alone will give you a head-start on understanding how mutual funds can help you if your goal is to accumulate wealth. It's my hope that the rest of the book will help you to understand a product that for many has made them richer than they ever imagined they'd be—mutual funds.

Much success with your investment choices,

Dian Vujovich
Mutual Fund Columnist

P.S. The three questions I'm asked most frequently about mutual funds are questions No. 1, No. 2, and No. 101.

Acknowledgments

I want to thank Steve Schoepke who reviewed the entire manuscript and helped me make sure the information was correct and clear. A. Michael Lipper and his firm Lipper Analytical Services helped me gather much of the data included in this book.

Dick Staron, Publisher at Chandler House Press, suggested I write this book and worked with me during its development. Jennifer Goguen guided it through the production process.

At CWL Publishing Enterprises, Kevin Campbell and Bob Magnan edited the manuscript, and John Woods designed and produced the final book. I want to thank them for their help.

Finally, thank you for investing in this book. I hope your return beats the market.

Part 1
Mutual Fund Basics

Jumping headfirst into the world of mutual funds without a clue as to what they are all about doesn't make a lot of sense. For openers, not only are there something like 8,000-plus funds to select from—with those numbers growing daily—but there are all sorts of little things you've got to know about a fund before ever investing a dime. Things like what they are, who manages them, and what they cost. Part 1 will walk you through those basics.

Question 1
What *is* a mutual fund anyway?

I sure wish there was a sexy, snappy, one-word answer to that question, but there isn't. That's because there is a lot more to understanding what a mutual fund is than grasping the implied meaning of those two words—i.e., "mutual" meaning "joint" and "fund" meaning "holding." So, while "joint holdings" isn't a bad way for brand-new investors to start thinking about these investment products that pool together lots of people's money and professionally manage it by investing that cash into a variety of securities, that definition doesn't tell the entire story. Why? Because what's held in a mutual fund portfolio frequently changes. So, they are often ever-changing investment vehicles. But there will be more about that later.

Technically, mutual funds are investment companies; and vice versa, investment companies are mutual funds. Both names are interchangeable. So, the next time you see the words "mutual funds" or "investment company," don't get confused; know that they both mean the same thing.

As companies, each and every one of the 8,000 or so different mutual funds out there has its own president, CEO, board of directors, staff, payroll, etc., and reason for being. A fund's investment objective will tell you the reason it was created. For example, some mutual funds have as their investment objective income, others capital appreciation, still others growth and income, and the list goes on.

Now that you know what a mutual fund is—an investment company that pools a number of people's money and invests it on their behalf with a specific investment goal in mind—and that each is a separate company with a mission statement known as an investment objective, you should know that one thing a mutual fund isn't is a guaranteed investment. All investments carry an element of risk. Consequently, don't expect a mutual fund investment to be any different from, say, an investment in an individual stock or bond in terms of return. There are no guarantees that the price of a company's stock will only go up in value or that a fixed-income security, like a bond, will be worth more than its face value before it matures. The same is true for mutual funds; there are no guarantees that these investments will make money for you during the time you own shares of them.

As far as their portfolios go, odds are that some of the holdings in your fund's portfolio will change each year. For instance, with money market mutual funds, the average maturity dates of holdings in their portfolios can't be longer than 3 months. Some stock funds try their best to hold onto the same stocks for years, while others turn their portfolios over throughout the year. Bond funds can change their portfolio holdings frequently as well. So, along with remembering what the technical definition of a fund is, remember too that although a fund's name usually remains the same year in and year out, what's in a fund's portfolio usually doesn't.

Question 2
What's it gonna cost me?

Bingo! And guess what? This is the second most frequently asked question about mutual funds.

Nobody works for free in the financial arena. And the costs fund shareholders are asked to pay can be divided into two groups: those that come right out of your pocket before any of your money goes toward buying fund shares, as in a fund's sales charge or its load, and those that are deducted from the fund's assets. These are referred to as a fund's *annual management fees and expenses*.

A fund's *sales charge*, or *load*, is akin to a commission. It's a one-time fee that gets paid to whomever sold you the fund for their work and effort. More than two-thirds of the funds out there have a sales charge. The ones that don't are referred to as *no-load* funds.

Load funds, however, don't all carry the same sales charge. The highest maximum sales charge found on a load fund these days is 8.50 percent. Twenty years ago, that was the going rate for loads. Now it's a rarity. Today, most load fees range from 3 to 6 percent, with those in the 3 to 4 percent range considered low-loads. Sales charges are levied—

- at the time you are investing in a fund. That means the load will be taken out before shares of the fund are purchased. These are referred to as *front-end load* funds; or
- when you liquidate your fund shares. In that case these funds will carry what's called a *back-end load*.

With each sales charge arrangement comes a specific class of fund shares: Class A and Class B shares.

Class A shares refer to funds with front-end load fee arrangements. This fee, as mentioned, is paid before any shares of the fund are purchased. Class B shares have back-end fees, sometimes called CDSLs, or contingent deferred sales loads. In this class, the sales charge isn't levied until shares of the fund are redeemed, i.e., sold. One cool thing about this charge, however, is that it may disappear over time. So, if you're a shareholder of a fund with a CDSL, and hold onto those shares long enough, when redeeming the shares, there might not be a sales charge imposed. You'll find detailed information about how long you need to be a shareholder in a fund and not have to pay its load in the fund's prospectus.

Along with Class A and Class B shares comes an alphabet of classes of fund shares, including some available only to institutions, others only for employees of fund families. What's important for you to focus on when deciding between classes of fund shares is—

- understanding the kind of sales charge arrangement the fund you're interested in has
- what precisely their costs mean to you

The fees that folks have to pay each and every year that they are shareholders of a fund include the fund's *annual management fees and expenses*, which typically run about 1.5 percent per year, and quite possibly, a *12b-1 fee*. While you won't write out a check for either of these fees each year, they will automatically be deducted from your account and impact the total return of your investment.

Money for a fund's annual management fees and expenses gets used to pay for the everyday things it takes to run an investment company, such as paying office salaries, renting office space, paying for the phones and electricity, and printing prospectuses. The 12b-1 fee, named after a Securities & Exchange Commission rule adopted in 1980, is used to pay for all sorts of things, including sales and marketing expenses and payments that no-load fund families make to bro-kers/advisors selling the fund.

The 12b-1 fee typically ranges between 0.25 and 1.25 per-cent annually. But, unlike other asset-based fees such as a fund's management fee, this one has a cumulative cap of 8.5 percent. That means, if the fund's 12b-1 fee is 1 percent annu-ally, after you've been a shareholder in the fund for more than 8½ years, you won't be subject to paying this fee anymore. In this way, a 12b-1 fee resembles a load, or sales charge.

Not all funds charge 12b-1 fees to their shareholders. To find out if a fund does—and the annual percentage amount charge—consult the fund's prospectus or Profile prospectus.

Add together the annual management fees and expenses along with a fund's 12b-1 fees and you'll have the fund's *total operating expenses*, sometimes called a total expense ratio.

A fund's sales charges and fee structures need close attention. What might at first blush look to be an inexpen-sive fund could turn out otherwise.

Who Is the Typical Mutual Fund Owner

At year-end 1997, 37.4 percent of all households—or about 65.5 million individuals—owned shares in mutual funds, according to research from the Investment Company Institute (ICI), the Washington, DC-based trade association for the mutual fund industry.

Other ICI fund research shows:

- Nearly 60 percent of folks owning mutual funds have household incomes ranging from $25,000 a year to $74,999.
- Most people owning mutual funds are between the ages of 25 and 64.
- The more money one makes the more mutual fund accounts they are likely to have.
- And, more households are likely to own equity funds than bond funds.

Question 3
Who manages the money I invest in a mutual fund?

Professional money managers called portfolio managers do.

Each mutual fund, i.e., investment company, hires a portfolio manager or assembles a team of money managers to invest the assets that come into the fund and all securities in its portfolio.

A fund's portfolio manager may be a man or a woman, young or old. If a team is managing the fund, its makeup could be any combination of people. Investment companies even hire firms and individuals outside of their fund families to manage funds for them, too. So there are all sorts of arrangements that can be made when it comes to who is managing your fund's money.

The Business Structure of a Typical Mutual Fund

SHAREHOLDERS

Board of Directors
Oversees the fund's activities, including approval of the contract with the management company and certain other service providers.

Mutual Fund

Investment Advisor/ Management Company
Manages the fund's portfolio according to the objectives described in the fund's prospectus.

Distributor
Sells the fund's shares, either directly to the public or through other funds.

Custodian
Holds the fund's assets, maintaining them separately to protect shareholder interests.

Independent Public Accountants
Certify the fund's financial reports.

Transfer Agent
Processes orders to buy and redeem fund shares.

Source: ICI

Question 4
How much risk is involved when investing in mutual funds?

That all depends upon a bunch of things, including the type of fund you've invested in and what's been happening during the time frame over which you've held your fund investments.

Risk, in the *Barron's Dictionary of Finance and Investment Terms*, is defined as a "measurable possibility of losing or not gaining value." Risk has been a very real part of the U.S. investing arena ever since the first stocks were traded in Philadelphia in 1790 and exchanged under a buttonwood tree in New York City in 1792.

While there are all sorts of investment risk—interest rate risk, political risk, inflation risk, exchange rate risk, etc.— the one that impacts the psyche of investors most is the one called "risk of principal," i.e., the chance that you'll lose some of the money you invested.

Because there are a variety of different types of mutual funds to invest in, from money market mutual funds to sector funds, there are also a variety of levels of risk to principal theoretically represented by each.

Money market mutual funds are considered to be the least risky fund investments for a number of reasons. First, the assets in these funds are only invested for a short period of time—the average maturity date on a money market mutual fund's portfolio by law can't be more than 90 days—

and a short holding period is considered to be less risky than
a long one. Another reason money markets are considered
safe has to do with what kinds of securities are in the fund's
portfolio. The safest funds are those that have only U.S.
Treasury securities in their portfolios. And finally, these
funds are designed to maintain a stable net asset value of $1
per share whether you are purchasing or redeeming shares.

Move out of money market mutual funds into all other
types of mutual funds and you've moved from investing in
short-term mutual funds, i.e., money market mutual funds
only, into a world made up of long-term funds, i.e., every
other type of fund. In this sphere, investors need to be
mindful that they are taking on more risk with their money
than they would be in money market-only fund investments.

If you're willing to risk some of your principal, here's a
broad brush look at how some of the largest types of funds
would rank if the least risky were considered 1, and the most
risky 8:

1. money market mutual funds
2. short- and intermediate-term bond funds
3. long-term bond funds
4. balanced funds
5. growth and income stock funds
6. growth stock funds including international/global funds
7. aggressive growth stock funds
8. specialty stock funds

Don't forget, that's just a broad look. In volatile markets,
all bets are off as there's often no telling what type of long-
term mutual fund will offer the most stable return. For instance, after a very rocky three-quarters of a year, by the end
of September 1998, it wasn't balanced funds, up nearly 2 percent, with the best year-to-date stock fund performance for the
year, but European Region funds, ahead by nearly 6 percent.

Knowing that principal risk is very real, and that most
folks would rather have their money working slowly for them
and at minimal returns rather than have it go down in value,
it's best to figure that along with any investment you make

into a long-term mutual fund comes a businessman's chance that over the course of your investment holding period, its principal value will decline at some point or other. And maybe just not once, but a number of times.

So, you could see the long-term net asset value of your fund fall the day, a month after, or years after you've made your first fund investment. When and why it happens is anybody's guess. How it will affect you will depend upon how prepared you are for taking principal risks.

Question 5
Can I be a mutual fund investor and not take any risks with my money?

Not really. For the money market mutual fund investor, the risks historically have been close to negligible. But for long-term fund investors, there's another story.

Decide to be a long-term mutual fund investor and you've taken your first step into the world of long-term money-making opportunities. And that opportunity comes at a cost—one that centers around risk.

It would be oh-so-sweet if there were only one kind of risk to be concerned with but, as you've probably figured out by now, risk is a multi-colored four-letter word and there isn't just one kind of risk, there are a number of them.

Two risks long-term domestic stock and bond fund investors need to understand are the risk of principal and interest rate risk. Here's what each means:

- **Risk of principal.** This is the big one and it means that there is a chance the money you've invested will drop in value. Various types of stock and bond funds carry different principal risks—some more, some less than others. So, you'll need to read a fund's prospectus, advertising material, and different fund resources to find out where the fund(s) you're interested in stand on the risk meter.

- **Interest rate risk.** For fixed-income fund investors,

that is, those who buy bond funds, a change in interest rates means a change in the value of a bond. In a nutshell, when interest rates go up, the prices on bonds go down, and vice versa. Any change in interest rates then plays with the overall value of your bond holdings.

Investors also have to be aware of the risk associated with inflation. That's a risk most often realized when you do the price-remembering thing and find yourself saying things like, "Gee, last year that loaf of bread cost me $1.25. Now the same loaf is $1.50."

Inflation risk might just be the cornerstone for investing in the first place. Why? Because prices on goods and services have historically gone up over time. So, to have enough money in the future to cover any rising costs, your money needs to be working for you at a rate at least equal to the rate of inflation—if not higher. And investing may provide you with those kinds of returns.

If you decide to invest in funds that invest in companies located outside of the United States, other risks come into play. Because no other country on the globe has stock exchanges as sophisticated and regulated as those in the U.S. are, investing in global, international, emerging market and country funds means—with a principal risk—you'll be taking on social, economic, political, exchange rate, and liquidity risks. Each of them is a reflection of how well their country is managed.

In the final analysis, investing and risk taking go hand in hand. And anyone who tries to tell you otherwise is pulling your leg.

Question 6
Why can't I just invest in money market mutual funds and forget about taking on any stock market risk?

You sure can do that. But the problem Wall Street types see with it is that because of inflation, over time your money won't have much buying power.

Getting a steady and constant yield from a money market mutual fund is one thing. But after paying taxes on that income—if your money is invested in a taxable money market account—it might not leave much once inflation is factored in.

Lately, the inflation rate has remained low in this country. Even so, it can make the value of a buck seem to disappear in almost no time as the following chart shows. In 1996, the inflation rate was 3.1 percent. At that rate, the value of $1,000 becomes $730 in only 10 years.

Here's how a 3.1 percent inflation rate works over other time periods:

In this many years	$1,000 will be worth
5	$854
10	$730
15	$624
20	$533
25	$455
30	$389
35	$332
40	$284

(Source: ICI)

Question 7
How important is it that I read a fund's prospectus?

In a word, very.

A mutual fund prospectus will bring to light all sorts of information that you're not likely to uncover from your broker, financial advisor, or from researching on your own. And, while this legal document might not be as inviting a read as say, *Lolita*, it's a whole lot more important from a financial point of view.

Fund prospectuses have also gotten the go-ahead from the SEC to become more reader-friendly, too. On June 1, 1998, that regulatory agency passed something called the "modernized Form N-1A" allowing fund prospectuses to be written in a more understandable fashion. That means you can expect to find less legal jargon and more conversational English in upcoming fund prospectuses.

But no matter what style a prospectus is written in, and no matter how long it takes you to slug your way through reading it, the time you spend doing so will be time well spent. No other fund document will be as informative as its prospectus in telling you things such as the reason the fund was created, the investment strategies it plans on using, the kinds of investments it can and cannot invest in, the risks of investing in the fund, who manages the fund, and how to buy and sell fund shares.

You'll also find out what all the fees and expenses of the fund are, see its past performance on a bar chart, and be able to compare that performance with the performance of an index representing the same kinds of investments as those that are found in the fund's portfolio.

So, to pass on reading a fund's prospectus is to pass on a very valuable learning experience.

I'd suggest first-time fund investors get a fund's prospectus before they invest; read that prospectus with the document in one hand and a yellow marker in the other so that you can highlight the words, concepts, and sentences that you don't understand; then, ask your broker, financial advisor, or fund representative to clarify the highlighted data.

Doing that will not only provide you with a wonderful free financial education, but will also clue you in to the nuts and bolts of the mutual fund investing world.

If you don't want to read a fund's prospectus in its entirety, make sure to read all of its Profile prospectus. And after doing that, don't even think about making a mutual fund investment until you know the answers to the following 13 questions:

1. What's the full name of the mutual fund you're investing in?
2. What family is it from?
3. Who is the fund manager?
4. How long have they been managing the fund?
5. What's the investment objective of the fund?
6. What kinds of securities, e.g., stocks, bonds, cash, are in the fund's portfolio?
7. What kind of sales charge and annual fees and expenses does the fund have?
8. How are fund shares bought and redeemed?
9. What has the fund's performance been like over the past 5 or 10 years?
10. How does that performance compare with an index of like investments?
11. What kind of return do you expect from the fund?
12. How long do you plan on holding it?
13. And, most importantly, why are you investing in the fund?

Question 8
I find prospectus reading dull as dirt. Can't I learn all I need to make an informed investment decision from these new Profile prospectuses?

Nope. While a fund's Profile prospectus will clue you in to lots of things about a fund, it's no replacement for the fund's prospectus.

After hearing about it for years, investors now won't have to slog their way through lengthy prospectus reading to learn about a fund they have an interest in. Instead, they'll be able to read about the fund via a fund Profile.

Ever since 1995, the mutual fund industry has been talking about creating a newer, friendlier, and easier-to-read document that would encapsulate things like the investment objective, past performance, and expenses of a fund into one simple package. In the spring of 1998, the Securities and Exchange Commission (SEC) passed a rule permitting such a vehicle. It's called a Profile prospectus.

The notion of creating the simplified Profile prospectuses had to do with the fact that most people don't bother to take the time to read the prospectuses they're given. Not only did they consider them long and dull pieces of legalese, just as the question points out, but folks also said that they're such boring reading, reading one can literally put you to sleep.

While fund Profiles will in no way wipe full-blown prospectuses off the map—they'll still be available, and if you don't get one before you purchase shares in a fund, you're definitely supposed to receive one after you've made your investment—the Profile prospectus will cut down on the reading wannabe investors will have to do in order to make informed investment decisions. And it's informed investors that the SEC, and the fund industry, hopes to see more of.

"Just a few years ago, observers wondered how investors would ever sort out the dizzying array of mutual funds being offered, then climbing toward the unprecedented figure of one thousand," said Arthur Levitt, the Securities and Exchange Commission Chairman in a Tuesday, March 10, 1998, meeting of the U.S. Securities and Exchange Commission. "Today there are more than 8,000 funds to choose from. That's more than double the number of companies listed on the New York Stock Exchange."

Levitt goes on to say that a Profile's "strict presentation of information can promote meaningful comparisons among funds," which in turn can help make investors' choices less daunting and more manageable.

With more funds coming out each year, and more and more investors having to learn about them so that they'll be able to make wise retirement and personal portfolio investment choices, it's hard to argue with the concept. As a result, most everyone agrees that the fund Profile makes good sense and will increase the readership of prospectuses from nothing to something.

Peter Brown, a partner with Evensky, Brown, Katz and Levitt, financial advisors in Coral Gables, Florida, likes the Profile prospectus idea.

"I think it's good because it might encourage people who wouldn't read the big prospectus to read this," he says. "But this is not an issue of 'a little knowledge is a dangerous thing.' It's that a little less knowledge is better than no knowledge at all."

If you want to learn about the mutual fund investment that you're about to make, reading a fund's prospectus is a must, as is reading its Profile prospectus; quarterly, semiannual, and annual reports; statement of additional information; and all the newsletters and additional information the fund family sends you. It's your money and the only one responsible for how that money goes to work for you is you.

The Profile Prospectus: 9 points to ponder

A fund's Profile prospectus allows investors to get a quick glimpse at many of the particulars of the fund they are interested in. And, while not a substitute for the real thing—the fund's prospectus—many say that the nine specific subjects covered in each Profile provide enough information for investors to make an informed decision about whether or not to purchase shares of that fund.

Here's a review of the nine subjects that absolutely positively have to be covered in a Profile prospectus:

1. What are the fund's goals? That means, what is the fund's investment objective—growth, income, etc.?
2. What are the fund's main investment strategies? In other words, what investment strategies does the fund intend on using to achieve its investment objective?
3. What are the main risks of investing in the fund? Here you'll find plenty of information about the risk of investing along with ideas about for whom this fund might be an appropriate investment. There is also a bar chart showing the fund's annual total returns over 1-, 5-, and 10-year periods along with the returns of an appropriate broad-based market index for the same time period.
4. What are the fund's fees and expenses? Here the fund's fee table will be shown.
5. Who are the fund's investment advisor and portfolio manager? Look for their names here.
6. How do I buy shares of the fund?
7. How do I sell shares of the fund?
8. How are the fund's distributions made and taxed?
9. And, what other services are available from the fund? You'll find things like wire transferring information and 24-hour telephone numbers listed here.

Question 9
Why do I have to own a mutual fund in the first place?

You don't. However, odds are if you now, or ever, work for a company offering any qualified retirement plans such as a 401(k), some of the investment choices those plans are likely to offer will include various mutual funds.

Funds also are popular choices for people's individual retirement accounts like their IRAs, Roth IRAs, SEP-IRAs, or Keogh accounts. They also are an appropriate fit in many personal portfolios. And they are an easy way to get your feet wet in the investing market without having to ante up tens of thousands of dollars.

Because of their versatility—and popularity—it's wise to learn as much as you can about mutual funds for two reasons. First, so that you'll be aware of what this investment product does and does not offer. And second, so that you'll be prepared should you one day find yourself in the position of having to decide which of them to invest in.

Question 10
How can a mutual fund make me any money?

A couple of different ways. First, the fund's per-share price, or its net asset value, can rise above the price it was when you first purchased your shares. When that happens you've made money. When the price is lower, a loss has occurred.

A fund's net asset value, or *NAV*, is calculated each day by the fund and reflects the fund's per-share price minus things like fund expenses and any *front-end load* fees—for example, a front-end load exists on Class A fund shares. So, keeping an eye on your fund's NAV will tell you how your investment is paying off.

Another way a fund can make you money is if the securities in a fund's *portfolio* pay dividends or interest. Those, as well as any profits from the sale of a security held in the fund's portfolio, get passed on to you, the fund *shareholder*.

Question 11
How do I know if a fund is going to make me any money or not?

With the exception of money market mutual funds—in which the net asset value is always supposed to stay fixed at $1 per share whether you are buying or selling shares—you don't.

Long-term mutual funds—those include everything from growth to fixed-income funds and exclude money market mutual funds—offer their shareholders lots of things, including professional money management in a diversified portfolio of securities within a highly regulated industry, an ability to invest in a broad array of securities for a fraction of their market cost, and the ability to get into and out of that investment quickly. But the one thing they can't promise is that you'll make any money.

So what does it take to make money from your long-term mutual fund investments? Good luck, good timing, good sense, smart asset allocation, and remembering the following:

- When folks talk about all the money that they've made in mutual funds, many times they are talking about money that they've made on paper, or about how their account values have increased in value since their initial investment. But in the end, paper profits aren't worth a hoot, and it is only realized capital gains that count. (A realized capital gain can only happen when shares of a fund are sold at a profit.)

- You can research a fund to death and know all about its portfolio manager, the manager's history, what his or her management style is, what's in the fund's portfolio, and things like the fund's beta, Sharpe ratio, expense ratio, and risk profile—but if the portfolio manager hasn't selected the right investments for the current market's mood, or you haven't purchased and sold your fund shares at a fortuitous time, your chances of making money are pretty slim. Mutual funds are investments, after all, and investments come with no guarantees.

Question 12
The portfolio manager on my fund is changing. What does that mean to me?

Sometimes a change in fund portfolio managers goes unnoticed and the new fund manager invests with the same style and into similar kinds of companies as his predecessor. Other times a change in fund management can mean a big shake-up in the types of companies represented, the style of management, and the numbers of securities held in the fund's portfolio. In short, the answer to that question is: only time will tell.

Read through any of the mutual fund industry publications and you'll see that portfolio managers changing funds or moving from one fund family to another happens regularly each year.

Knowing that change is a natural part of the money management business, here is what some industry experts think investors ought to do when they realize that a change in their fund(s) portfolio management is imminent:

- **Barbara Levin**, executive director of Forum For Investor Advice, a Bethesda, Maryland nonprofit association serving full-service financial advisors, suggests that investors talk with their brokers or financial planners once they learn of a change in a fund's portfolio management before doing anything drastic—like selling their fund shares.

  "The hope is that your financial advisor will be sufficiently in touch with the fund company and know the importance of any portfolio management changes," says Levin.

- **Sheldon Jacobs**, editor of *The No-Load Fund Investor*, said that 90 percent of the time a change in portfolio managers means nothing to the fund's shareholders. "It's like any job, if somebody quits they replace them with someone else and more often than not the replacement is as good as the guy that quits."

  He added that the 10 percent exception to that won't come from the large fund families but from the smaller families where one star money manager stands out. "If you're invested in something like the Van Wagoner funds and Garrett got run over by a truck, that's another story because I know there is nobody there but him."

- **Maria Scott** is editor of the *AAII Journal*, an educational and investment publication based in Chicago.

  The American Association of Individual Investors (AAII) recommends that investors find out all they can about a fund manager's style before initially investing. That way, when a change in portfolio management happens, investors will be one step ahead of the game when researching and comparing what a change in their fund's portfolio management could really mean.

  Scott said that fund companies try to keep an orderly transition and will try to keep a similar investment style. So, she wouldn't necessarily pull out of a fund just because the manager has changed.

Here are some questions that will help you to evaluate what a change in a fund's portfolio manager could mean:

1. Is the portfolio manager being replaced by someone of equal or greater experience?
2. Is the departing manager a star portfolio manager or one of a team of managers?
3. Did the new portfolio manager train and work with the old one, or did he or she come from another fund or fund family? If so, what is his or her background?

4. What is the reason for the change? For instance, is it a result of the fund merging into another fund family, poor performance, or what?
5. Does this change mean that there will be any changes in the fund's style of management? If so, how so?

Remember, change doesn't necessarily mean bad things for shareholders—it can mean good things, too.

Question 13
What does "long-term" mean?

Great question! And thanks for asking, because long-term has a couple of faces that need identifying.

To the Investment Company Institute (ICI), the trade association for the mutual fund industry, a long-term mutual fund is any fund other than a money market mutual fund. The same is true for ranking and rating companies such as Lipper Analytical Services, Morningstar, and Value Line.

But, when one is talking to industry representatives—like a portfolio manager or fund representative—oftentimes when they talk about "the long-term" what they are referring to is a holding period, i.e., how long to hold onto a fund before it can be expected to start making you any money. FYI, their answer is typically 3 to 5 years.

When I ask someone on the street what long-term means in holding period terms, answers range from a few months to years. Or it can stretch out decades.

Ask me what I think long-term means, and as far as holding periods go, it means decades to me. From a how-long-do-I-need-to-hold-on-to-a-fund-before-I-can-expect-it-to-make-me-any-money point of view, I believe one ought to consider staying invested in a mutual fund for the bare minimum of 5 years. If someone can't commit to that, I say money market mutual funds are the best choice. After all, the performance numbers I see show that you don't make the real bucks in funds until 5, 10, 15, and 20 years out.

Question 14
What does "short-term" mean?

Short-term, like its long-term cousin, has a couple of meanings.

Money market mutual funds are often referred to as "short-term parking places" for money. The thinking behind that reflects the short maturity dates of the securities held in a money market's mutual fund portfolio. It also reflects the fact that these funds serve as a convenient place to put money while deciding where or how to invest it for the long term.

You'll also find "short-term" being used in title form. There are any number of long-term fixed-income mutual funds using "short-term" in their names. The meaning of those two words in this case has nothing to do with how long you ought to own that investment. Rather, it's an indication of the maturity dates of the securities held in the fund's portfolios.

Question 15
Other than a sales charge, like load or no-load, what other fees and costs come with the fund?

Fund fees and expenses can be mind-boggling both for newcomers and for those who have been investing in funds for decades. They exist because an investment company—which is another name for a mutual fund—has to have capital to run, pay its employees, and promote its product: the mutual fund.

What each fee means as it appears in a fund's prospectus will be listed below.

But before going there, there are six things to remember when it comes to understanding a fund's fees and annual expenses:

1. All funds—whether they are load or no-load funds— have annual fees and expenses that they charge their shareholders.
2. Annual fees and expenses affect the total return you get from your investment—they reduce it. So, the higher a fund's total expenses, the less gain that means for you.
3. Some fees are taken directly from your investment, others are deducted from the fund's assets.
4. Never assume that the fees and annual expenses from all funds within the same family of funds will be identical. They won't be.
5. A fund's fee and expense tables are always listed in the fund's prospectus and also in its Profile prospectus.

6. Once a fund has been established, changing its management or 12b-1 fees requires a vote from its shareholders.

As point 3 states, some fees are taken out of your investment dollars, and others are deducted from the fund's net assets. The list below describes how the fees in each group shake out. Those taken directly from your investment dollars include the following:

- **Maximum sales charge.** This is what's called a "front-end load." It's a charge deducted from your initial investment. Federal law allows front-end loads up to 8.5 percent, although very few funds charge the legal limit. Front-end loads are expressed as a percentage of the fund's offering price.
- **Maximum sales load** is imposed on reinvested dividends. This is a fee charged by some funds on dividends that are reinvested in the purchase of additional shares. Most funds don't charge this fee.
- **Deferred sales load**, also called a "back-end load," refers to a sales charge that is paid when you sell shares of a fund. Contingent deferred sales charges (CDSLs) are one type of back-end load. Under this type of load, if you sell shares during the first year of ownership, you are charged a fee of up to 6 percent of the amount sold. The fee decreases each subsequent year until it disappears.
- **Redemption fees.** Charged on shares held less than 90 days, this is like a short-term trading fee and may be expressed as a dollar figure or as a percentage of the amount redeemed. A redemption fee is paid to the fund and is not a sales charge.
- **Exchange fees.** Excessive switching of your investment from one fund to another within the same mutual fund family often has a cost. So, while many funds allow their shareholders a few free exchanges a year, after that the fees typically run between $5 and $25 per switch.
- **Account maintenance fees.** These are annual fees that some funds charge, usually to maintain low-balance accounts.

Now for the fees that aren't as obvious. These are deducted from your fund's assets. So, even though you can't see
them being subtracted from your account as you can in the
fees mentioned above, they are there and include:

- **Management fees.** This yearly fee is paid to the fund's
  investment advisor for managing the fund.
- **12b-1 fees.** Not all funds charge these fees. Of those
  that do, some charge this fee to compensate investment
  professionals for selling and promoting mutual funds.
  Others charge 12b-1 fees to pay for distribution and marketing expenses. If any do, a fund may not charge more
  than 0.75 percent of average net assets per year for distribution and marketing. A fund may also charge a service fee of up to 0.25 percent of average net assets per
  year to compensate sales professionals for providing services or maintaining shareholder accounts. These service
  fees can be in the fund's 12b-1 fee; so, 12b-1 fees can be
  up to 1.00 percent. Funds that charge 12b-1 fees above
  0.25 percent may not call themselves no-load funds.
- **Other expenses.** Here costs can include the costs of
  fund services, such as toll-free phones and customer
  service, computerized account services, record-keeping,
  legal printing, mailing, or advertising.
- **Total operating expenses.** This is the sum of all the
  fund's annual operating costs. It's expressed as a percentage of average net assets. Total operating expenses
  are also known as the fund's expense ratio.

As you can see, there's a lot to a fund's costs and expenses. Make sure that you're always aware of each before ever
investing in a fund. A fund's annual fees and expenses, as I
pointed out, all impact the return you get. So, whether you're
investing in a fund via your company's 401(k) plan, in your
own retirement portfolio, or in your personal account, make
sure to look at a fund's expenses and then compare it to
other like funds for competitiveness. Again, it's your money.
Spend it wisely.

Question 16
How much is too much to pay in annual fees and expenses?

A good rule of thumb is around 1.5 percent. If a fund's annual expenses are running much higher than that, say over 1.75 percent, better reconsider. There are plenty of top-performing, well-managed mutual funds—and fund families—that have kept their expenses under control and at the same time have done a good job for their shareholders. The most well-known are the large no-load fund complexes that try to keep their annual fees and expenses around 1 to 1.25 percent per year. So there's really no need to pay caviar prices for fund investing.

Understand the Fund's Expense Ratio

A fund's expense ratio can have a big impact on the long-term total return you get. To illustrate how very important it is to investigate a fund's expenses before you invest, check out this example from the Investment Company Institute booklet, *Frequently Asked Questions About Mutual Fund Fees*:

"Consider $10,000 investments in two funds. The first fund has an expense ratio of 1.10 percent. The second fund has an expense ratio of 1.74 percent. Both funds have annual returns of 10 percent a year on their portfolios before taking fees into account. The investment in the fund with the lower expense ratio would grow to $302,771 in 40 years. The investment in the second fund would grow to $239,177, or $63,594 less than the first fund."

I'll admit that 40 years is a mighty long time to hold onto a mutual fund. But fees start to make a noticeable difference after 10 years of fund ownership. So look at them closely. They count.

Question 17
What part does the capital gains tax play in my fund investing?

Sometimes a lot. Sometimes a little. One of the mutual parts of being a mutual fund investor is that each year there's the likelihood that you'll have a capital gains tax to pay on your fund investments.

You get that privilege because mutual funds—by law—must distribute all capital gains and dividend income to their shareholders. So, you don't have to sell any of your fund shares to trigger a capital gains tax. Just being a shareholder is enough.

If you are a tax-sensitive investor and are confused by the various levels of capital gains taxes and the part they play in your mutual fund investing scheme, remember these two points:

- First, people who own individual stocks are subject to a capital gains tax only when they sell their securities. Mutual fund shareholders face the likelihood of capital gains taxes annually.
- Second, it's the amount of time a security is held that triggers the different capital gains tax rates, with the longer holding periods being the most tax beneficial. For instance, assets held from 12 to 18 months are taxed at the maximum capital gains tax rate, which currently is 28 percent. Stretch that holding period out for over 18 months and the rate drops to 20 percent. For assets acquired after the year 2000 and held for at least 5 years, the maximum rate will then be 18 percent, or 8 percent for people paying income taxes at the 15 percent rate.

Question 18
I don't know the difference between a fund's total return and its yield.

Both are ways to measure performance. And both are terms you need to know the meanings of, because they will show you how well your fund is doing and will also provide a way to compare performances among like funds.

A fund's *total return* reflects the changes in the value of the assets held in a fund along with any income it produces. Expressed as a percentage, this figure shows how a particular fund—or fund category—has performed over a given period. Plus is to the good. Minus, to the not-so-good.

At the end of September 1998, for instance, the average growth fund had a total return of 0.21 percent, according to Lipper Analytical Services. That means from December 31, 1997 through September 30, 1998, the average growth fund's net asset value (NAV) had gone up less than a quarter of one percent in value. In other words, growth funds on average didn't make their shareholders much money during the first nine months of that year.

A fund's total return can be calculated for all sorts of different time periods. Consequently, when comparing total return performance numbers, make sure to look closely at the dates of the time periods expressed to insure that you'll be comparing apples to apples.

A fund's yield—also expressed as a percentage—shows

the dividends and interest, less expenses, that have been earned in a fund's portfolio over a given time. Income investors, like those investing in bond funds who take regular payouts from them, along with money market mutual fund investors, are typically most interested in a fund's yield.

When comparing yields, make sure to also double-check the time frame used.

Both yield and total return are ever-changing.

Question 19
How do I tell how much money I've made from my fund last year?

By looking at the fund's total return and doing some very simple math.

I know that lots of people say they have difficulty reading their fund statements, and about how to figure out if they are really making any money. But finding out whether you are or aren't making money isn't as intimidating as it may seem to be. It's really quite elementary.

Below is an example the Janus family of funds used in one of their educational booklets entitled, "Getting There." (If you'd like to see what else is in that kit, it's free for the asking from Janus. Call 1-800-525-8983 for your copy.) It's a good example because, along with showing how to figure your fund's total return, it also assumes that a fund's distribution into it gets plowed back into the fund to purchase more shares of it, which, by the way, is what most people do with the distributions they receive.

Here's Janus's example of how to calculate a fund's one-year total return:

- Your initial investment of $2,500 on 12/31/97 at a net asset value (NAV) of $25 buys 100 shares. You plan to reinvest all income dividends and capital gains distributions.
- By 12/31/98, the NAV has risen to $30. On that same day, a distribution of $1.10 per share is paid. ($0.10 per

share income dividends and $1.00 per share capital gains.) The NAV automatically drops to $28.90 ($30 NAV minus $1.10 distributions).

- With your total distributions of $110 (100 shares multiplied by $1.10 per share), you reinvest at $28.90 to buy an additional 3.806 shares. You now own 103.806 shares. At the current price, your investment is worth $3,000.
- By subtracting the beginning account balance ($2,500) from the ending balance ($3,000) and dividing the result ($500) by $2,500, you get a one-year total return of 20 percent.

If you are to use that example as a guideline, figuring out how your fund investment has worked for you over a 12-month period ought to be relatively easy.

As you can see, there is more to making money than merely having some cash and picking a fund—adding, subtracting, multiplying, and dividing are part of the deal, too.

The Bottom Line on a Fund's Per-Share Price

A fund's net asset value (NAV) represents the per-share price of the fund, minus fund expenses, including a front-end sales charge if the fund happens to be a load fund.

This dollars-and-cents figure is usually calculated every day after the market closes. Because it's a daily calculation, a fund's NAV will move with the market.

Doing the math to find out a fund's net asset value is relatively simple. Here's how:

- Add up the market value of the securities held in the fund—let's pretend that all the stocks, bonds, and cash in Mary Mary Quite Contrary's Fund total $8 million.
- Subtract the expenses of that fund, say $80,000, from that $8 million.
- Divide that figure—$7,920,000—by the number of investor shares outstanding. Let's pretend there are 1 million shares outstanding in this fund. So, the NAV of this fund on the day it was calculated would be $7.92.

Question 20
What's a bear market?

Some pros say it's when the market falls by 20 percent. Others say when it falls by 25 percent.

Bear markets are a natural part of a market's personality, just as flat and bull markets sometimes are.

While there's no telling when a bear market will appear, or end, there is data showing how previous bear markets have impacted various types of mutual funds.

The following is from Lipper Analytical Services and looks at various rolling 12-month periods along with the number of months it took for different fund types to recover from their bear market losses.

Remember, the past performance of fund types is no indication of how they will perform in the future.

Rolling 12-Month Period 12/31/86 Through 12/31/97 Worst Three Months		
TYPES OF FUNDS	% Return	Months to Recover
General Equity Funds		
◆Cap Appreciation Funds	-29.93	22
◆Growth Funds	-29.20	18
◆Mid-Cap Funds	-33.91	21
◆Small-Cap Funds	-33.17	20
◆Growth and Income Funds	-25.79	16
◆S&P 500	-29.66	18
◆Equity Income Funds	-22.78	14

TYPES OF FUNDS	% Return	Months to Recover
Sector Equity Funds		
◆Health/Biotech Funds	-33.82	19
◆Natural Resource Funds	-32.36	44
◆Science and Tech Funds	-35.95	29
◆Utility Funds	-11.20	13
◆Financial Services	-27.45	14
◆Specialty	-35.06	28
World Equity Funds		
◆Gold Oriented Funds	-33.65	76
◆Global Funds	-25.06	21
◆International Funds	-23.58	20
◆European Region Funds	-25.49	29
◆Pacific Region Funds	-28.54	27
Mixed Equity Funds		
◆Flexible Portfolio Funds	-16.02	16
◆Global Port Funds	-13.15	15
◆Balanced Funds	-18.15	14
◆Convertible Securities Funds	-21.35	21
◆Income Funds	-15.30	11
Source: ICI		

Question 21
Any suggestions about the kind of attitude I need before I make my first mutual fund investment?

A positive one.

If you believe in corporate America and that the prices of company stocks will increase over the long term, then stocks will probably be a good asset class choice for you. If you don't see things that way or don't want to weather the uncertainty of how a stock fund's net asset value changes, then this asset class might not be the best place for you to invest.

One of the things I've learned during all the years of my reporting about mutual funds is that stock fund managers are positive thinkers. No matter what the market conditions are, they can see some form of opportunity either in the near or long term. They believe in their product, i.e., stocks, and they've got to. It's their job.

Your job is to invest in things that you see value in— stocks, bonds, real estate, gold, original art works, whatever. Then, continuing to learn about those investments will help improve the odds that you'll make some money from then.

If you're brand new to the investing world, chances are that you're already an optimist—but a starry-eyed one. A study from PaineWebber Inc. conducted in July 1998 showed that inexperienced investors expect more from their investment returns than more experienced and seasoned investors do. They are also more confident about their ability to beat the market averages. On both of these scores, it would pay if the newcomer paid more attention to those with more investing experience.

Anyone who's been an investor in mutual funds for the past 10, 15, 20 years or more knows that it is very hard to wind up with a portfolio of mutual funds in which the collective performance numbers beat the averages.

Part 2
Fund Types

Just as each of us has our own body type and personality, mutual funds do, too. Knowing that some funds are designed to provide income, others growth, and still others a combination of the two not only helps you to learn more about the varieties of mutual funds, but also helps when selecting the types of funds needed to meet your specific investment goals. You'll learn about the various mutual fund types and their differences in Part 2.

Question 22
There are all sorts of mutual funds. How can I know what each one is and if it's one I ought to be investing in?

You're right. There are plenty of different kinds of mutual funds out there, and trying to figure out which one(s) you ought to invest in isn't easy and depends upon what your goals are and the kinds of investments you'd like to make.

As you weed through the various kinds of funds, remember these three points:

1. All funds can fall under three main headings, each heading reflecting a different asset class:
   - *Money market mutual funds.* Included here would be all types of taxable money market mutual funds, including all-purpose funds, government and/or Treasury money market funds, plus all forms of tax-free money market mutual funds, including state and/or national money market funds.
   - *Stock/equity funds.* Here expect to find everything from large-cap stock funds to micro-cap ones, world, global, and international funds, and every type of specialty equity fund you can think of.
   - *Fixed-income funds.* Look for every type of bond fund imaginable here. That would include short-, medium-, and long-term bond funds; high-yield and high-quality taxable funds; tax-free national and state funds; international, global, foreign, and single-country

fixed income funds; and any other bond fund type in between.

2. Each fund has an investment objective that may or may not give you a clue as to the category that the fund falls under. A fund's investment objective is like its mission statement—it will give you an idea of the reason why the fund was created. For example, the Nicholas 11 fund, according to its prospectus dated January 1998, has a primary and secondary investment objective. The primary investment objective of this fund is "long-term growth, and securities are selected for its portfolio on that basis.... Current income will be a secondary factor in considering the selection of investments...," reads the prospectus. Based on that information, one might think this fund would be categorized as a long-term growth fund. But look for it in Lipper's universe and it is listed under their Mid-Cap heading.

3. There is no central clearinghouse that makes the carved-in-granite rules as far as defining the various types/categories of mutual funds. So, reading a fund's prospectus to find out the kind of investments it can make is Job 1 for all fund investors.

Add these three points together, and you can see that it takes more than merely reading investment objectives and category types to understand the fund(s) you'd have an interest in investing in.

I suggest investors go about finding a fund by—

- first looking at the asset class in which they'd like to invest,
- then examining the amount of risk they'd like to take,
- and finally, deciding for how long they plan on being invested.

Folks are often amazed at how the answers to those three questions can help whittle down the entire universe of mutual funds into something more manageable.

Then, once you can get your arms around an armful of fund choices—

- look at the fund's previous track record,
- then check to see if you believe in the future of the types of companies it holds in its portfolio and how the fund is managed,
- and decide whether its sales charges and annual fees and expenses are in line with what you're willing to pay.

Answering those questions ought to bring what once might have looked like a huge number of funds to select from down to a very few.

Mutual Fund Management Fees

Different types of mutual funds have different management fees. So, while the average mutual fund annual expense ratio is about 1.50 percent each year, management fees can vary depending upon the kind of fund you've invested in.

Here's a look at the average management costs for various types of funds from two sources, the September 1998 issue of *Working Woman* Magazine and the Summer/Fall 1998 issue of *Kemper Report*.

From *Working Woman*—they listed Lipper Analytical Services as their source—the average expense ratio numbers read as follows:

Category	Average Annual Expense Ratio
International funds	1.65%
Micro-cap funds	1.65%
Growth funds	1.52%
Mid-cap funds	1.48%
Small-cap funds	1.47%
Growth & Income funds	1.29%
S&P Index funds	0.52%

In the *Kemper Report*, Morningstar was the source for the figures they used regarding the average annual expenses of various fund types. Their numbers show:

Category	Average Annual Expense Ratio
General Bond funds	0.91%
Domestic Stock funds	1.40%
International Stock funds	1.84%

The moral of this story is when looking at the average annual expense ratio for an entire category of funds, always remember that those numbers are averages. The expense ratio on the fund you're interested in may in fact be higher or lower.

Question 23
What's the difference between growth and value stock funds?

Even though both invest in stocks and may invest in the stocks of companies of various sizes, managers of growth funds look to invest in companies that can predictably grow their earnings at a steady pace. Value managers look for companies that are relatively cheaply priced.

Growth fund managers assume that the products' growth companies make will not only be hot, but will continue to be big sellers into the future. Microsoft is an example of one of the biggest growth companies recently.

The challenge all growth fund portfolio managers face is twofold: identifying the growth companies, and buying them early. This allows for catching as much of their growth in stock price as possible.

Value fund portfolio managers, on the other hand, are looking for bargain companies, such as stocks of firms that may have fallen out of favor with the market for one reason or another. A good value company might be one in which a company's earnings growth isn't as great as it once was for reasons as simple as a change in market cycles. But price alone isn't enough for a company to be considered a good value buy. The company's balance sheets have to make sense, and since many of these companies are large-cap ones, some of their attractiveness also lies in the assets the company owns, how well it's managed, and the consistency of its dividend payouts.

Both types of funds add diversity to your fund portfolio. Which you invest in first depends a lot upon your style—do you like growth stocks or value ones?

Regarding performance, plan on these funds performing differently, because sometimes growth stocks are in favor and at other times value stocks are.

From December 31, 1997 through August 11, 1998, here's how various growth and income funds performed, according to research from Morningstar:

Capitalization size	Year-to-date through August 11, 1998
Large-Cap	
growth funds	+14.66%
value funds	+ 2.03%
Mid-Cap	
growth funds	+ 3.75%
value funds	− 3.08%
Small-Cap	
growth funds	− 5.37%
value funds	− 6.71%

Question 24
What's a balanced fund?

It's a fund for those who want to play both sides of the market and invest in both stocks and bonds.

Balanced funds have been around since the late 1920s. With well over 400 funds in the category, this two-pronged approach to mutual fund investing appeals to market newcomers, the less aggressive, and the seasoned investor.

The investment objective of a balanced fund is to conserve principal by maintaining a balanced portfolio of stocks and bonds. Typically, these funds have about 60 percent of their portfolios invested in stocks and 40 percent in bonds. As far as performance goes, balanced funds have had an average annual total return of 12.40 percent for the past 15 years (9/30/83 through 9/30/98); 12.03 percent over the past 10 years; 11.66 percent over the past five; over 13 percent during the last two and three years; and 3.26 percent for the last year, according to Lipper Analytical Services.

Even though there is no way to tell how balanced funds will perform in the future, the fact that this type of fund has increased in numbers and assets shows that they have the ability to weather financial storms. While that may not sound really sexy, this fund type certainly has been enduring. For the first nine months of 1998, the average balanced fund was up nearly 2 percent, while the average general equity fund was down almost 5 percent. Over the past year, balanced funds were up 3.36 percent and over the last 5 years, over 45 percent. That compares with the general equity funds, down 6.33 percent and up almost 90 percent, respectively.

Question 25
What's the skinny on index funds? Are they really worth investing in?

Ten years ago, index funds were just beginning to get noticed. Today, with hundreds of them around, they represent a world of their own, some actively and some passively managed.

When most people think of index funds, they think S&P 500. But S&P 500 funds aren't the only index game in town. There are now index funds for large-, medium-, and small-cap companies; index funds for bonds and REITs (real estate investment trusts); index funds for domestic and international markets; and even index funds for indexes. Plus, some index funds are professionally managed to perform better than the index they follow. They are actively managed index funds.

"It's probably good that there are more index funds now," says Susan Dziubinski, editor of *Morningstar Fund Investor*. "Because it puts the spotlight on indices other than the S&P 500. And that's good because the market is not just the S&P 500."

With more than 200 index funds around, investors have exposure to almost every corner of the market. But the increase in fund choices only means that investors have to do more digging to find the one that's right for them.

In May 1998, for instance, Vanguard, the fund family that put index funds on the map, introduced three new equity index funds. They were the Mid Capitalization Stock

Portfolio (it seeks to parallel the investment performance of
the S&P MidCap 400 Index); the Small Capitalization Value
Stock Portfolio (it seeks to replicate the performance of the
S&P SmallCap 600/BARRA Value Index, which is made up of
380 stocks with lower-than-average price/earnings and
price/book ratios); and the Small Capitalization Growth Stock
Portfolio, which is designed to track the performance of the
S&P SmallCap 600/BARRA Growth Index (it is made up of 22
stocks with higher-than-average price/earnings and
price/book ratios).

These additions bring the number of index funds that that
family alone offers to twenty-five. Consequently, if you were
to ask for a prospectus on, say, their S&P index fund, it's para-
mount that you know which part of the S&P world you're
interested in.

But Vanguard isn't the only family offering index funds.
Many fund families, brokerage houses, banks, and insurance
companies offer them. So, the challenge for investors doesn't
really begin with whose index fund to buy but what kind to
invest in.

Given that most index funds are equity funds, figuring
out whether you'd like an index that follows large-, medium-,
or small-cap stocks is the first question that needs to be
answered.

Dziubinski thinks index funds representing large company stocks—like S&P 500 index funds—make a lot of sense
because "it's tougher for an actively managed large-cap portfolio manager to add value." The reason for this is that large-
cap stocks are so highly visible and well covered it's difficult
to find any surprise performance punch.

In the small-cap arena, it's just the opposite. With
many, many more stocks to pick from and less coverage on
the companies and their management, Dziubinski said that
"if you are looking for a small company fund, you might
actually want to look for an actively managed fund."

Once you've picked your market size, there's the choice
of index representation. S&P, Wilshire, and Russell all have
indices for various-sized stock companies.

Initial investment fees also vary on these funds. On the low end, Morningstar research shows 25 index funds with minimal initial investments of $1,000 or less available through brokerage firms such as Schwab, Principal, Transamerica, U.S. Global, MainStay, Domini, Victory, and Merrill Lynch.

Then there are annual expenses. Because index funds can be both actively and passively managed, costs need to be considered. The least expensive index funds will be those that are passively managed—computers there do all the work. Actively managed index funds—where there is a human manager's touch—are likely to cost more. As always, check into fund expenses, being ever mindful that the less they are the more you make.

As for performance results, don't expect much leeway: In passively managed index funds, the index that the fund you invest in follows will pretty much reflect the return you'll get. In an actively managed one, you ought to have better performance than the index but not by much—say a half of a percent or so.

Question 26
What's a mid-cap fund?

This is the middle child in the range of small-, medium-, and large-sized companies. It's also a fund category in which funds are invested in companies that aren't start-ups but have successfully grown from small companies into bigger ones.

In the world of growth funds, historically, the two company-sized categories investors generally think of right off the bat are small- and large-cap funds. But, thanks to phenomenal growth in corporate America recently, a number of small companies have enjoyed wonderful success and have grown into mid-sized companies. Hence, there are now mid-cap funds.

Go back 10 years, though, and you'll find no mid-cap fund category listed by Lipper Analytical Services. In fact, that category of funds didn't break out from the Lipper universe of growth stocks until the first quarter of 1994.

"One of the things we had noticed was that growth funds, at times, did not do as well as the S&P 500, or the Dow, " says A. Michael Lipper, chairman of the mutual fund research firm bearing his name. "When we looked into it, we found that some funds owned mid- or small-cap companies. So, the only fair thing to do was to separate the group. First, we split out small-cap. Then mid-cap."

In March of 1994, there were 77 mid-cap funds listed in

the Lipper mid-sized fund category. Assets totaled $26.3 billion. By the end of June 1998, the story had changed—there were then 341 mid-cap funds around with assets in them totaling over $91 billion. The mid-cap asset class provides an attractive alternative to the traditional small- and large-cap types of portfolios. And many not only perform better than small-cap stocks, some may also be less risky.

One reason mid-cap companies might outperform their small-cap cousins is because of size. Once a company makes it over that 1 billion-dollar capitalization marker moving it from the classification of small-cap to medium-cap, it is likely to be a company with good growth characteristics, a track record, seasoned management, and liquidity.

"When you have graduated from the first generation of management and products to the second, the company is taking on much more of the attributes of a public corporate body. And, it has to deal with more outside analysis," says Lipper.

Although nobody really wants to learn that growth funds have been sliced and diced yet another time, recognizing that many small companies do in fact grow into medium-sized ones—and medium-sized companies may grow into large ones—opens our eyes to new investment possibilities.

How Big Is Big?

Trying to keep a handle on what constitutes a small-, medium-, or large-sized company isn't easy. That's because what's considered big today—in terms of company capitalization—might be small ten years from now.

Market capitalization is the value of a corporation that's based upon multiplying the per-share price of stock in the company times the number of shares of common stock it has issued.

So, in the 1950s for instance, a company with a market capitalization of, say, $250 million, would have been considered a big-time company. Today, a company that size is considered a baby, as in micro-cap.

Based on June 1998 guidelines, here are the Lipper definitions for what constitutes the micro-, small-, mid-, and large-cap fund categories:

- Micro-cap funds invest in companies with a market cap of less than $300 million at the time of their purchase.
- Small-cap funds invest in companies with market caps of less than $1 billion at the time of their purchase.
- Mid-cap funds typically invest in companies with market caps of less than $5 billion at time of purchase.
- And, large-cap funds are made up primarily of companies with market caps greater than $5 billion.

Question 27
How about European funds? I understand they're hot these days. Why?

The European stock markets started to pick up steam at the end of 1997. At that time, stocks in the U.K. were up 23 percent; Germany, up 25 percent; France, ahead 12 percent; and Denmark, up 35 percent, according to research from U.S. Trust.

That upward trend in prices continued into 1998, resulting in some impressive returns for shareholders whose funds invested in the European region. Through May 28, 1998 the average European Region fund had gained 27.31 percent, according to Lipper Analytical Services. For the previous 52 weeks, the category was up on average 36.34 percent. And, over the previous five years, it had an average total return of 20.93 percent.

Rory Powe, head of INVESCO's European equity team in London, said that one reason for the surge in European stock prices was low inflation.

"German and French inflation is today nearer 1 than 2 percent," said Powe, whose team selects the stocks that go into the INVESCO European Fund portfolio. "But the major change as far as inflation is concerned takes place in southern Europe, where inflation today is just over 2 percent. Four years ago it was in excess of 5 percent."

Other reasons for the strong European stock markets include investor interest and corporate restructuring. First, there is investor interest. Along with low inflation has come a low interest rate environment. And, with an aging population that faces the same do-I-have-enough-money-to-retire dilemma that Americans do, Europeans—historically fixed-income investors—are now beginning to turn to the stock market rather than the bond market in hopes of funding their retirement years.

Rosemary Sugar, manager of the U.S. Trust Excelsior Pan European fund, says that this is in the beginning of an up-cycle for investors as Europeans are acquiring an appetite for stocks.

On the corporate side, she thinks that Europe's market strength is the result of a major cost-cutting and restructuring trend similar to that experienced by U.S. companies earlier in this decade. And Powe agrees, pointing out that European companies have been going about improving their profitability in the same ways the U.S. companies did 5 and 6 years ago. He said that they are focusing on productivity and operational efficiencies using technology to drive those efficiency gains and outsourcing activities that formerly were done internally.

One new fund to focus on in the European scene is John Hancock's European Equity fund. Its portfolio manager, Jean-Claude Kaltenbach, said that in addition to the current investor-friendly environment of historically low inflation and low interest rates, the advent of the European Monetary Union (EMU) in 1999 and the euro in 2002 could propel markets further.

But not all news in Europe is rosy. Unemployment, for instance, is very high. In France and Germany, Powe said it is in excess of 11 percent. And then there is the European Monetary Union. No one knows the real impact it will have on markets until after it goes into effect on January 1, 1999.

All of which makes investing in European funds risky and best for those with long-term time horizons.

FYI, one hundred funds make up Lipper's European Region category. Included in that number are single-country funds. Top performers from December 31, 1997 through May 28, 1998 included:

- WEBS Spain fund, up 43. 20 percent;
- AIM's European Development fund, up 42.86 percent;
- WEBS Italy fund, ahead 39.12 percent;
- Smith Barney World Europe fund, up 37.31 percent.

Question 28
Why have all the world equity funds performed so miserably lately?

Not all have. European Region funds were up almost 6 percent for the first nine months of 1998 and international small-cap funds were ahead 0.60 percent.

Aside from Europe and international small-cap funds, some of the reasons for the world equity funds' poor performance include the high cost of capital, slower economic growth, and investor sentiment.

Sentiment, as the money pros will tell you, is what drives markets. And a lot of what has happened in markets around the world in 1998, they say, was as much sentiment-driven as anything else.

While there is no telling how mutual funds in any fund category from domestic to global will perform in the near term, lessons from the market meltdown in the summer of '98 can remind us that:

- *Markets change.* For economic, political and emotional reasons, stock and bond markets are dynamic environments. Things are ever-changing and pretty much need to be if money is to be made.
- *Mutual funds are long-term investments.* Excluding short-term money market mutual funds, funds are typically best suited for people who plan on having their money invested for 5 years or more. Over the last 5 years, domestic general equity funds have had an aver-

age annual total return of 13.65 percent and over the last 10 years of more than 14 percent. Global funds, on average, have returned over 10 percent on average for the past 5 and 10 years.

- *Investing in various asset classes and fund types provides a cushion during volatile market conditions.* Having money invested in cash equivalents, like money market mutual funds, as well as various types of stock and bond funds, means that you might not get the highest return possible, but you won't get the lowest, either.
- *There is a difference between an emerging market, an integrating market, and a developed market.* Neil George, international funds director at Guinness Flight funds, reminds investors that not all emerging markets are alike. Some represent new governments and/or new economies, like those in countries such as Russia, Malaysia, and Indonesia. Other countries have markets that have moved out of an emerging status and integrated themselves with first world economies. Examples here include countries like the Czech Republic, Slovakia, and Poland. Developed markets include the U.S. and Western Europe.
- *Even in down times, not all funds are losers.* Two top-performing funds in August 1998 were the Profunds: Ultrabear Investors fund, up 34.10 percent for the month, and the Prudent Bear Fund, ahead 31.29 percent. Year-to-date winners that month included the Montgomery 11: Global fund, up 35.10 percent, and AIM Intl: Euro Development fund, ahead 31.23 percent.

Question 29
Are municipal bond funds still a good investment?

Usually yes, if your tax bracket warrants.

It's no secret: tax-free municipal bond investing, i.e., munis, aren't for everyone. But, if you find your income tax bill from Uncle Sam levied in tax brackets ranging from 28 percent on upwards, chances are muni bond funds might provide you with more income than, say, taxable bonds could.

For instance, a tax-free municipal bond yielding 4.5 percent is equivalent to a taxable yield of 6.25 percent for someone in the 28 percent tax bracket. For an investor in the 39.6 percent federal income tax bracket, the muni deal is even sweeter; the equivalent taxable yield there would be 7.45 percent.

Municipal bond funds come in a variety of flavors. Some are state-specific, investing in only the tax-free bonds of one state; others are national, investing in bonds from all around the country; some have portfolios made up of bonds with similar maturity dates, like short-, medium-, or long-term muni bond funds do; and some represent combinations of those just mentioned. There are even muni funds that only have insured bonds in their portfolios, or high-yielding ones. In other words, for every high net worth investor's needs, there's probably a municipal bond fund that's right for them.

Although investors who opt for short- or medium-term

muni funds give up the luxury of obtaining the higher yields that a long-term fund pays. In a changing interest rate environment, that choice means they also aren't likely to be faced with as much per-share price volatility, either. And, in the intermediate-term muni funds, bond experts say that investors get to pick up 90 percent of the long-term yield with two-thirds of the volatility.

But making sure your tax bracket warrants a tax-free investment is only part of the story. Investors need to do a little homework before jumping into any municipal bond fund. Along with looking at the tax-free taxable-equivalent yields on these funds, they need to do things like consider the tax structure of their state if they are looking at state-specific muni funds; check to see if the fund has any bonds in its portfolio that will subject them to the Alternative Minimum Tax (AMT); consider the capital gains taxes the fund has kicked off in the past; and investigate the fund's expenses—the lower they are, the better off you'll always be.

Question 30
What's the big to-do about tax-managed mutual funds?

It's all got to do with giving less to Uncle Sam.
In tax-managed mutual funds, which can be made up of either stocks or bonds, portfolio managers invest with an eye toward the long term, trying to minimize the trading of the securities held in the fund's portfolio. That way, when a fund makes its annual capital gains and dividend distributions, hopefully, the tax bite shareholders are faced with will be minimized.

One of the reasons "tax-managed" has become a real buzzword in the fund industry lately is because many folks are tax-sensitive, preferring to pay Uncle Sam as little tax on any money made from their investments. So, a fund that invests with a tax-managed point of view looks pretty sweet to some.

Russel Kinnel, an equity fund editor at Morningstar, says that there are some funds that haven't made any capital gains and dividend distributions to their shareholders since their inception. "They essentially have won their shareholders a big advantage," he said.

Steven Norwitz, a spokesperson at T. Rowe Price, illustrates the benefits of investing in tax-managed funds. He says that if you had $20,000 in a fund not managed for taxes, the fund had a net asset value of $10, you owned 2,000 shares of it and got a $2 per share capital gains and dividend distribution, that would mean a $4,000 distribution. "Even if it's all taxed as a long-term capital gain, it's still $1,120 in taxes (based on a 28 percent rate) that you'd have to pay," he says.

But there's at least one downside to tax-managed funds. Funds like this can rack up a lot of unrealized capital gains over time. So, just because your fund advertises itself as a tax-managed one, don't think you're skirting the long arm of the Uncle. When fund managers sell any of the stocks that have gone up substantially in price over the years, come year-end when the fund passes on its capital gains tax responsibility, shareholders could be hit with a handsome capital gains tax.

According to Morningstar, there are only a few dozen funds keeping a specific eye on being tax-managed. My guess is, you'll hear more about this from many more funds in the future. But be mindful here: If tax management is your primary reason for investing, a better option might be buying individual stocks. That way, it's you who controls when the capital gains tax gets paid and not a fund manager.

Question 31
What's an equity REIT?

An equity REIT (Real Estate Investment Trust) is a company that owns and actively manages a portfolio of real estate, like hotels, apartment complexes, and commercial and retail properties.

Equity REITs, by law, have to distribute 95 percent of their income to avoid paying corporate tax. So, one of the reasons investors and fund managers like them is because they can kick off a nice yield.

Another reason they are popular is because they are stocks and have upside performance potential.

Robert Benson, portfolio manager of the Pioneer Real Estate Shares, said that in early 1998 the real estate market represented about 17 percent of the U.S. economy. And that over the last 20 years, equity REITs have returned on average more than 16 percent per annum, making them attractive long-term growth vehicles. But along with these impressive average annual returns on these stocks have come some pretty volatile times.

Before investing in a fund made up of equity REITs, investors would be wise to investigate a real estate fund's holdings to get an idea of the kinds of REITs the fund invests its assets into—like commercial, office or industrial real estate, or condominiums, full-service hotels or resorts—and have a feel for the real estate market. The reason being, anyone who has ever followed the real estate market knows that it runs in cycles affected not only by interest rates but also by geographic and local economic conditions. And therein lie the bulk of the risks related to equity REIT investing.

Question 32
All of a sudden, it seems as if everyone is talking about hedge funds. What are they?

A Hedge funds are for big hitters with big bucks looking for big returns of one kind or another. And, thanks to the bulge in the number of wealthy individuals who have made bundles in the stock market over the last few years, the numbers—and total assets—in these funds have grown.

Hedge funds are like mutual funds in that they are investments in which a number of people pool their money and hand it over to professional money managers who invest it into a host of securities for them. But, that's about as far as the similarities go. Hedge funds, you see, aren't regulated by the Securities and Exchange Commission as mutual funds are. Nor do their portfolio managers have to be registered. All of which means they'll often use investment strategies that mutual fund managers aren't permitted to use or stay away from because they are considered too risky.

Hedge funds also aren't available to everyone as most open-end mutual funds are. Investors must have major money both *to* invest and *in* net worth. It's nothing for hedge funds to insist that their shareholders earn at least $200,000 a year; have a net worth of at least a $1 million; and ask for minimum initial investment requirements ranging from, say, $100,000 to $1 million or more. Having said all of that, if you fit the profile, these funds can provide some big returns on both the plus and minus side.

Look deeper into hedge funds and you'll see that the really big money often goes to their portfolio managers. That's because they often have performance-based fees, unlike open-end mutual funds, and the annual fees and expenses on hedge funds are typically much higher than those on regulated mutual funds. For example, the average management for a mutual fund runs about 1.50 percent a year, whereas hedge fund managers might earn a 1 to 3 percent annual management fee, plus fees up to 25 percent of the fund's profits.

Question 33
I've heard there are mutual funds that trade on the stock exchanges just like stocks do. What are they?

They are closed-end funds.

Closed-end funds, formally named closed-end publicly traded companies, are a cross between a mutual fund and an individual stock.

Like a stock, closed-end funds trade on both the major exchanges and the over-the-counter markets, with their per-share price depending upon supply and demand, as all U.S. stock prices do.

Like a mutual fund, closed-end funds offer professionally managed portfolios made up of a host of different companies following various investment themes. Some of the more popular ones are single country and municipal bond funds.

What sets closed-end funds apart from their open-end cousins centers around the number of shares each makes available: Like all publicly traded companies, closed-end funds issue a specific number of shares of stock. Once those shares begin trading, the per-share price for them, again, depends upon supply and demand. In order for you to purchase any shares of a closed-end fund, there have to be sellers who make the shares available. That, however, is not the case with open-end funds.

Open-end mutual funds issue shares upon demand. Consequently, there is no end to the number of shares a mutual fund company can have outstanding. So, when someone decides to purchase fund shares, they don't have to wait for someone else to redeem, i.e., sell, any. Open-end fund shares can be redeemed any business day at the fund's net asset value (NAV). Remember, a fund's net asset value is calculated by looking at the value of all the securities in the fund's portfolio, minus fund expenses, and divided by shares outstanding.

Because of the differences, buyers of closed-end funds need to be aware of a couple of things before investing. The first is the fund's per-share price, which is what's quoted in newspapers and seen on stock screens. The second is net asset value. (To find out that figure, ask the closed-end fund folks.) It's important to look at both numbers, because the NAV will tell you whether the fund's per-share price is trading at *par*, at a *premium*, or at a *discount* to its NAV.

A closed-end fund whose stock is trading at par is one in which the NAV of its underlying portfolio is equal to the fund's per-share price. One that's trading at a premium to its NAV means that its per-share price of the stock is higher than the value of all the securities in the fund's portfolio. One trading at a discount to its NAV means that the value of the portfolio is greater than the stock's per-share price.

Another difference between open- and closed-end funds is commissions. Because closed-end funds trade like stocks, there are commissions to be paid when both buying and selling your fund shares.

Question 34
How many different closed-end funds are there?

Over 500, according to the Closed-End Fund Association.

For information about any of the fund offerings, and data on how to contact them, here's the address:

Closed-End Fund Association
P.O. Box 28037
Kansas City, MO 64188
Voice: 816/413-8900
Fax: 816/413-8999
E-mail: cefa@cefa.com

Question 35
What makes variable
annuities so attractive?

Three reasons for the big appeal of these products, which are essentially mutual funds with insurance wrappers around them, are:

• There is no limit to the amount of money that can be invested in a variable annuity.

• Earnings on the money in them can grow tax-deferred, usually until the owner is age 85, and in some cases until age 100, before it has to be annuitized.

• And, you can have a guaranteed income stream for life from these insurance products should you choose. (Keep in mind, if you die before the lifetime income feature of your variable annuity runs out, the remaining balance doesn't go to your beneficiary. Instead, the monies go back to the insurer.)

Variable annuities, however, are riddled with fees and expenses. In addition to the annual management fees the underlying mutual funds charge, some insurance company-related fees include annual mortality and administrative fees. Then there are surrender charges levied on those who decide to cash out of their policies before a given date. All of which put a drain on your total return.

At The Vanguard Group, a no-load fund family that offers variable annuities with some of the lowest annual fees and expenses in the industry, a representative said that it's "very

very important" to pay close attention to annual fees. Why? Because despite the tax advantages, if you're paying around 3 percent in fees on an annuity each year, the fees are so high that those tax advantages become almost meaningless.

On the other hand, other insurance pros say that fees are a small price to pay if you're getting good performance from this investment.

While both points are valid, would-be investors need to remember that variable annuities are both expensive and long-term investments.

"Expect to stay invested for 20 years or it (a variable annuity) doesn't pay," says financial author Alan Lavine.

Question 36
I'm concerned about having too much money in annuities. I've put money into them, and wonder how much is too much?

Finding out if you've got too much money in annuities is a tough question to answer. That's because there are so many variables to consider as each individual invests for different reasons and with different amounts of money. So, the best way to find out if you've got too much invested in annuities is to sit down with a tax professional and/or your certified public accountant, and let the figures do the talking. And your investment goals determine how much money you ought to allocate to them.

A spokesperson from the National Association of Variable Annuities (NAVA), said that there is no limit to the amount of money one can put in an annuity during the accumulation phase. But he warns that people ought not put 100 percent of their money into annuities only. That's akin to keeping all your eggs in one basket, and we all know the potential perils of that strategy.

 **Question 37**
Are annuities advisable at
my age? I am 80 and my
wife is 72.

That's a tough question to answer, mainly because no one knows how long they are going to live. But the industry pros I spoke with said that the real question you ought to be asking here is not about age but about what your intended use of the money is.

If the money in your annuity is to be used as a source of your retirement income, then they might fit the bill. But, if you want to pass this money on to your heirs, annuities are probably not the best way to accomplish that. The pros say that individual mutual funds might be a better choice. The reason for this is the tax consequences levied on variable annuities and the high annual fees they impose.

As far as the "how old is too old" part of the question, my insurance gurus tell me that a person needs to be invested in an annuity for about 10 years before any of the tax advantages offset the annual fees.

Question 38
Where can I find basic information regarding variable annuities?

One of the best places to start is their trade association, the National Association of Variable Annuities (NAVA). They offer a number of brochures available free for the asking. Contact them at

NAVA
12030 Sunrise Valley Drive, Suite 110
Reston, VA 20191
Voice: 703/620-0674
Fax: 703/620-6362
Web: www.navanet.org

Part 3
Performance

If you've ever wondered why folks invest in mutual funds, the answer is simple: performance. Buy shares of a mutual fund and you're hoping to make some money. Right? But not all funds make money for all their shareholders all the time. Part 3 will provide you with a snapshot of how various types of mutual funds have performed in the past. Which, by the way, is no guarantee of how they will perform in the future.

Question 39
My husband says that if the stock market falls, so will my fund, no matter what kind of fund it is. What do you think?

I think that depends.

If the stock market were to dive deeply and stay in negative territory for months or even years on end, your husband would no doubt be correct. But, if it were to fall then flatten out or seesaw its way back up, it's possible that your stock fund could miss the blow of the drop.

The best example of that is what happened in 1998 as the stock Dow Jones Industrial Average headed south after hitting its all-time high figures in mid-July. Mutual fund performance numbers from December 31, 1997 through August 6, 1998 showed that only about one-third of funds lost money during that time period. The hardest-hit category was small-cap funds. Below is a chart showing how the numbers stacked up over that time frame.

Investment Objective	Number of Negative Funds	Number in Category	Percent of Negative Funds
Small-Cap	510	604	84.4%
Micro-Cap	34	45	75.4%
Mid-Cap	144	317	45.4%
Capital Appreciation	65	240	27.1%
Equity Income	58	215	27.0%
Growth	133	981	13.6%
Growth and Income	91	742	12.3%
S&P 500	0	86	0.0%
All General Stock Funds	1,035	3,230	32.0%

Source: *The Wall Street Journal*, August 10, 1998

With Each New Year Come New Performance Expectations

In an Oppenheimer survey of 551 investors conducted in November 1997, investors were asked what kinds of returns they expected from their fund investments in 1998. Five percent expected the annual return on their investments to increase by 25 percent or more in 1998; 17 percent expected an annual increase of 15 percent but less than 25 percent; about two-thirds thought that the value of their stock portfolios would increase between 5 and 15 percent; and 10 percent thought the stock market would be lower at the end of 1998 than it was in 1997. While the jury is still out regarding those expectations and market realities, the best performance rule of thumb for fund shareholders to follow is a historic one. History has shown us that the long-term result of fund investing is similar to the long-term result of investing in individual stocks, bonds, and cash instruments. Here's how the numbers look:

	TIME PERIOD	
	35 Years	10 Years
	Beginning 12/31/60	Beginning 12/31/85
Fund Type	Ending 12/31/95	Ending 12/31/95
Growth Funds	10.62%	13.41%
Small Company Growth	12.24%	14.02%
Growth and Income	11.05%	12.78%
Balanced Funds	9.78%	11.47%
Long-Term Fixed Income	7.97%	8.87%

Source: Lipper Analytical Services, Inc.

Question 40
Anybody ever lost big money in a mutual fund?

Yes. And recently.

While folks were getting the kids ready for school this past August, world-wide markets were in a free fall, with Russia seemingly leading the way. On August 27, 1998, funds investing in Russia, Latin American, and emerging markets experienced phenomenal one-week losses. Here's a tiny example of some of those losses:

Name of Fund	Drop in Total Return in One Week from 8/20/98 to 8/27/98	Year-to-Date Total Return
Lexington Troika Russia Fund	-23.10%	-83.83%
INVESCO: Latin American Growth Fund	-20.79%	-50.25%
Fidelity Latin American Fund	18.68%	-46.92%
Smith Barney World Emerging Markets	-17.16%	-47.09%

But just because these funds were losing money for their shareholders during that week in August doesn't mean every single fund out there was or that those losses translated into year-long ones. For example, through August 27, 1998, the Prudent Bear fund was up 61.36 percent for the year; the

Grand Prix fund ahead by 40.20 percent; Potomac OTC Plus fund up 39.01 percent; and Fidelity's Select Computer fund was up 37.53 percent.

For a reality check, never forget that risk is a very real part of investing.

The Big Fall

From July 17, 1998 through September 3, 1998, the stock market experienced its biggest fall of the decade. For stock funds, that market drop meant that most funds lost all of the gains they'd made for the year.

Growth and income funds are considered "moderate." But, as the numbers below show, when the market dives, all stock funds—even those considered not to be as risky as others—can fall right along with it.

Here's a look at how the 5 largest growth and income funds in America weathered that late summer storm:

Name of Fund	Percent Fall Since Peak 7/17/98 to 9/3/98	Year-to-Date Total Return 12/31/97 through 9/3/98	12-Month Total Return 9/3/97 through 9/3/98
Washington Mutual Inv	-13.09%	-0.17%	+7.71%
Investment Co. of America	-14.11%	+0.53%	+4.74%
Fidelity Growth and Income	-15.91%	+2.48%	+8.62%
Vanguard Windsor II	-17.14%	-2.79%	+3.83%
Vanguard Windsor	-24.52%	-14.23%	-16.09%

Source: Lipper Analytical Services, Inc.

Question 41
I'm 21 years old, and my parents tell me that when they were young, the stock market wasn't a very good place to put your money. Are they right?

Your parents are right. On two occasions, once in 1969-1970, and then in 1973-1974, the stock market lost roughly half of its value and stock prices didn't recover from the latter fall until 1982. So, even though the really long-term historical picture shows that the general trend of the market is up, there have been years and even decades when that's not been the case. The ones just mentioned are a perfect example of how it can take years for stock prices to recover. That's why it's so important to follow the old "don't put all your eggs in one basket" philosophy. Over the life of one's long-term investing program, no one knows for sure which investments will pay off the most—stocks, bonds, or cash.

FYI, here are some market history tidbits worth thinking about before beginning your investing journey. The data is from Fidelity's Personal Finance Review 1998 booklet titled *Your Finances: An Owner's Guide.*

- Stocks have lost money in 20 calendar years out of the past 72.
- It took 15 years for investors to get their money back after the 1929 crash.
- On average, the stock market declines 10 percent or more every 24 months. There have been 12 of these "corrections" since 1970.

- A bear market—when prices drop 25 percent or more—
  has happened on average every six years this century.
- Forgetting the averages, from 1970 through March 1998,
  there has been
  a 5 percent dip in stock prices 38 times;
  a 10 percent dip 12 times;
  a 15 percent dip in prices 7 times;
  a 20 percent dip 5 times; and
  a 25 percent, i.e., bear market, dip 4 times.

Please note: These figures were calculated on data collected
before March 30, 1998.

The Chances of Profitability

The sweet thing about investing in stocks is that the
research shows the longer a stock is held, the greater the
chance there is of its being a profitable investment.

For example, according to research from Standard &
Poor's, between 1926 and 1995, if stocks were held one day,
they had a 52 percent chance of making money. If they
were held one year, there was a 71 percent chance they'd
make money. Extend that to five years, and there was a 90
percent chance of making money. Hold on for ten years,
and you had a 97 percent chance of making money.

While those numbers are impressive, keep in mind that
stocks don't always make their shareholders money.

(Source: The Securities Industry Association booklet,
Understanding Market Risks: What Every Investor Should Know.)

Question 42
How fast can things change on Wall Street?

Sometimes very fast. At other times, not so fast. On August 31, 1998, the Dow Jones Industrial Average fell 535 points. Add that one-day loss to the losses ticked off over the previous six weeks and the Dow and S&P 500 wound up down over 19 percent, wiping out all they'd gained for the year.

A friend of mine likened that August 1998 fall to a diet. "Geez, it's like you work and work all year long trying to lose weight, and in six weeks you blow it. Everything you lost gets put back on again," she said. And she's right. Stock market gains that seem as though they've taken eons to obtain can be wiped out in a day, a week, a few months, or even through the years.

What's been wiped out can also take days, weeks, months, or years to regain. For instance, after the stock market hit a high in the mid-1960s, it started a downward trend from which it took nearly two decades for prices to return to their '60s highs.

The point to focus on through any market, however, is not how well the market is doing, but how well your personal investments are doing. To do so, consider the following:

- If your funds have fallen precipitously in value, do you have a long enough investment time horizon for them to hopefully pick up steam again?

- Does the change in market atmosphere mean you need to rethink your investment strategy? or rebalance your portfolio? perhaps invest in more fixed income rather than equity funds, or vice versa?
- Or, is it time to cash out of some or all of your long-term funds and move the money into interest-bearing ones like money market funds?

The market affords everyone investment opportunities all the time, no matter what the conditions are. But it is up to everyone, once they've decided to play the stock and bond market game via mutual funds, to find the funds that meet their investment needs and manage the money they've invested in them to meet their own personal money objectives.

After all, the money you have to invest in mutual funds is money you manage and are ultimately responsible for. To be a satisfied fund investor you need to remember that.

As you can see, investing in mutual funds comes with some challenges. Before you buy your first long-term fund share, better ask yourself if you are up for those challenges. If not, perhaps it's best to become—or remain—a saver. Savers make money too, you know.

Question 43
How much has the stock market dropped in one day?

A lot, as the charts below show.

Here's how much the Dow Jones Industrial Average has dropped in any one day:

Date	Point Drop	Percent Drop
Oct 19, 1987	508	22.61%
Oct 28, 1929	38.33	12.82%
Oct 29, 1929	30.57	11.73%
Nov 6, 1929	25.55	9.92%
Dec 18, 1899	5.57	8.72%
Aug 12, 1932	5.79	8.40%
Mar 14, 1907	6.89	8.29%
Oct 26, 1987	156.83	8.04%
Jul 21, 1933	7.55	7.84%
Oct 18, 1937	10.57	7.75%
Feb 1, 1917	6.91	7.24%
Oct 27, 1997	55.26	7.18%
Oct 5, 1932	5.09	7.15%
Sept 24, 1931	8.20	7.07%
Jul 20, 1914	7.32	7.07%
Jul 30, 1914	5.30	6.91%
Oct 13, 1989	190.58	6.91%
Jan 8, 1988	140.58	6.85%
Nov 11, 1929	16.14	6.82%
May 14, 1940	9.36	6.80%
Oct 5, 1931	6.29	6.78%
May 21, 1940	8.30	6.78%
Jul 26, 1934	6.06	6.62%
Sept 26, 1955	31.89	6.54%
Aug 31, 1998	512.61	6.37%

What to Expect from the Market

Want to know what to expect from the market? Here's a look at how portfolios made up of individual stocks and individual bonds have fared from January 1945 through December 1997. Use them as a guideline when thinking about the kinds of long-term returns to expect from your stock and bond fund picks.

Portfolio	Compound Annual Total Return	Worst Year's Return	Number of Years with Losses of...		
			5%	10%	20%
100% Stocks	12.9%	-26.5%	8	4	1
80% Stocks/20% Bonds	11.6%	-20.5%	8	2	1
60% Stocks/40% Bonds	10.3%	-14.3%	3	1	0
40% Stocks/60% Bonds	8.8%	-7.9%	1	0	0
20% Stocks/80% Bonds	7.3%	-3.9%	0	0	0
100% Bonds	5.8%	-5.1%	1	0	0

Source: *The Wall Street Journal*, September 8, 1998 and Ibbotson Associates.

Question 44
Over the past year, how much has the stock market gained in one day?

Plenty. Ranked below are the 10 biggest plus move days of the Dow Jones Industrial Average based on point moves, from September 1997 through September 9, 1998.

Rank	Date	Point Change	Percent Increase
1.	Sep 8, 1998	350.53	4.98%
2.	Oct 28, 1997	337.17	4.71%
3.	Sep 1, 1998	288.36	3.82%
4.	Sep 2, 1997	257.36	3.38%
5.	Nov 3, 1997	232.31	3.12%
6.	Feb 2, 1998	201.28	2.55%
7.	Dec 1, 1997	189.98	2.43%
8.	Oct 21, 1987	186.84	10.15%
9.	Apr 29, 1997	179.01	2.64%
10.	Sep 16, 1997	174.78	2.26%

Question 45
Are index funds really good performers?

They have been.

According to Nations Funds in Charlotte, North Carolina, research on unmanaged index funds shows the following:

- The S&P 500 beat most mutual fund managers in 1994 through 1996.
- Out of 289 mutual funds surveyed from 1980 through 1984, only 63 outperformed the S&P 500 Index.
- From 1966 through 1975, the median pension fund stock portfolio returned 1.6 percent, versus 3.3 percent annually for the S&P 500 Index.

Performance numbers like that are the reason billions have poured into S&P 500 Index funds over the last few years.

Question 46
My cousin invested in a fund that returned her over 40 percent last year. Is there a fund that will do that every year?

The performance of any mutual fund is not guaranteed. Year after year, a fund's total return (that's a combination of the change in a fund's net asset value and any dividend or interest income it earned) depends upon a number of things. The three basic ones are:

1. *The market.* If a fund is investing in stocks, for example, and stocks have had a lousy year, don't expect big-time returns from a stock fund. If it's a bond fund, how interest rates have changed throughout the year will impact the return on fixed-income funds, too.
2. *The securities held in the fund's portfolio.* A fund can only be as good as the various securities that are in its portfolio. So, regardless of the asset class that's winning the "make money" race in a year, a fund's portfolio has to be packed with the right stuff to be a winner.
3. *How well the fund is managed.* If stocks are running hot one year, you can still have a stock fund that isn't performing well. Why? Perhaps the portfolio manager had invested the fund's assets into different sectors of the market that didn't perform well that year. Or they sold their positions too soon. Or too late. Or, the fund was too diversified. Or not diversified enough.

Because of all the variables, don't expect any of your mutual fund investments to provide you with a consistent return year after year. That's not the nature of the markets, or of the performance of mutual funds.

Question 47
How long do bear markets last?

History shows that the bears can hang around for anywhere from a few months to more than 25 years.

While there have been plenty of bear markets in U.S. stock market history, below are figures showing how long the previous ones have lasted.

Date of Market Peak	Percent Decline	Years to Return to Peak
Jul 16, 1990	-21.2%	0.75
Aug 25, 1987	-36.1%	2.0
Apr 27, 1981	-24.1%	1.5
Sep 21, 1976	-26.9%	4.5
Jan 11, 1973	-45.1%	9.8
Dec 3, 1968	-35.9%	3.9
Feb 9, 1968	-25.2%	6.8
Dec 13, 1961	-27.1%	1.75
May 29, 1946	-23.2%	3.9
Sep 3, 1929	-47.9%	25.2

Source: *The Wall Street Journal,* September 3, 1998

Question 48
It seems like this bull market has gone on forever. I know that good or poor fund performance runs don't last forever. So, about how long does a stock fund cycle last?

Sources at Lipper Analytical Services report that most equity investment cycles last four to five years. And over the last 150 quarters, general equity fund performance has been down for 46 quarters and up more than 5 percent for 66 quarters. Also, since 1959, there has not been one instance of 20 percent gains for three consecutive 12-month periods.

"History does not have to repeat itself, but the odds favor some return to past experiences," says A. Michael Lipper, chairman of a mutual fund research firm bearing his name.

That quote was made before the market hit the skids in 1998. At the end of the third quarter 1998, stock funds were at their lowest performance levels—for that one quarter—since 1990. And long-term fund performance numbers—like the total returns on fund types for the past 5, 10, and 15 years—were near their historic levels, typically around 10 to 13 percent, depending upon the type of fund.

Question 49
Is there anyplace I can get a quick run-down on the market's performance during this decade?

The library, the Internet, newspapers, magazines, TV, and radio programs are all sources for sound current financial information. And, so are fund families. Most of them offer a variety of educational material—all for free.

The Van Kampen American Capital family of funds, for one, has a brochure titled, "Bulls? Bears? How Much Do You Really Have To Care?" It includes some good basic information that new and experienced investors might find useful.

One of the booklet's bar charts, for example, shows the annual returns of the S&P 500 from 1990 through 1996. Because the data is presented visually, it's easy to see that in spite of a market that's been up most of the years shown, it has not been a market that lacked volatility. Here's why: In 1990, the S&P 500 (with reinvested dividends) was down 3.17 percent; in 1991, up 30.55 percent; 1992, up 7.67 percent; 1993, up 9.99 percent; 1994, ahead 1.31 percent; 1995, up 37.43 percent; and 1996, up 23.07 percent. So, even bull markets have their ups and downs.

You may request a free copy of this booklet by calling 1-800-421-5666.

Part 4
Strategies

If you want to accumulate money from your fund investments, it's best to have a plan. In the money arena, having a successful wealth-building plan generally means investing in stocks as well as bonds and keeping a rainy-day cash/savings account on hand. Part 4 will introduce you to the idea of asset allocation and diversification as well as help you to understand other investment strategies, like when to sell your mutual fund shares.

Question 50
What is asset allocation?

Asset allocation is an investment strategy that the pros say, if done properly, can help make you money because it may provide your investment portfolio with some shelter when the market is falling and reward you when it's going up. Plus, following the strategy will keep your risk/rewards parameters in balance, which in the long-run ought to help you meet your investment objectives in a fashion that you're comfortable with.

In its simplest form, asset allocation means investing money among the various asset and sub-asset classes. There are three big asset classes—stocks, bonds, and cash and/or cash equivalents—and then a bunch of sub-asset classes.

Since we've discussed the big three asset classes before, some of the categories of funds under each include growth and value, micro-, small-, medium-, and large-cap stock funds—plus, growth, growth and income, balanced, and index funds, and international and global funds, just to name a few. Sub-asset class fund headings get more specialty-oriented and include gold, single country, regional funds, and a host of others.

In the bond fund world, sub-category headings include funds that invest in short-, medium-, and long-maturing bonds. And those that invest in taxable and tax-free bonds. Some bond funds are state- or region-specific, others have national or international holdings.

For cash equivalents in the mutual fund arena, there are all sorts of sub-asset class headings, including national, government, Treasury, and tax-free money market mutual funds. Got that? Whew!

Question 51
I'd like some ideas on how to spread my money around: how much should I invest in stock and bond funds? And how much keep in cash?

That's the 64 million dollar question. What you're really asking about is asset allocation, the divvying up of money among the three asset classes. But more on that later. First, let's look at why it's almost impossible for someone—other than yourself—to answer the asset allocation question explicitly.

Because each of us has an entirely different amount of money to invest, similar but different personal goals, and uniquely different risk and reward tolerances, it's really difficult for anyone to tell you precisely how to divvy up your dollars. So, to help you get a clue as to how you'd like to do that, you need to learn about your investment choices, and the differences between stocks, bonds, and cash. Then decide things like how much risk you'd like to take and how you feel about investing in various products. To find out, you might want to spend time with an investment professional answering some questions and filling in answer forms so that a clearer picture of how you feel about investing emerges. Even then, the blend of asset mix he or she might suggest may be different than one that "feels" good or your instincts suggest is good for you.

If that sounds a little too right-brained, and you're not interested in how you "feel" about investing and just want the bottom-line facts on which assets will make you the most money, consider the following:

- *100% Stocks/Equities.* A portfolio made up of only stocks has the potential to provide you with the greatest overall reward over time, provided you've selected the right companies at the right time. The right companies means selecting ones that are making tons of money during the time frame for which you are invested. So, not only do you have to be a good picker, the time you stay invested in the market has to be the same time that that micro-, small-, mid-, or large-cap company (and that may be either a U.S., foreign, or emerging market company) that you've picked hits it big. Oh, lest you forget, just as a portfolio made up of 100% stocks can provide you with the biggest rewards, it can also provide you with the largest losses, too.

- *100% Short-, Medium-, and/or Long-Term Bonds/Debt.* A portfolio made up of only individual bonds will supply an income, provided the bond doesn't default, which something like 97 plus percent historically don't. Hold on to a bond until it matures, and you'll get interest from it each year that you own it, plus all the money back you originally invested. Unless, of course, you bought the bonds at a discount—in that case you'll get back more than what you invested. Or, at a premium—in which case you'll get back less. The risks in holding only individual bonds include income—it's fixed and it doesn't grow; the ability of the bond issuer to make timely interest and/or principal payments—which most do; inflation—which erodes the income's purchasing power; and price—should you sell your bonds before they mature, the price you get for them may or may not be the same as what you paid. The rewards are simple; you know what you've got and what it pays.

- *100% Cash/Cash Equivalents/Short-Term.* Things like CDs, savings bonds, Treasury bills, and money market mutual funds will always provide you with some kind of return. Whether that return amounts to much after you've paid taxes on it depends upon interest rates and your tax bracket at the time you have your money invested in them. On the other hand, there have been periods of time when savings vehicles like those just mentioned have outperformed the stock market. One of the most recent periods was January 1, 1998 through September 30, 1998 when the stock market lost all of its nine-month gains. And, in the late 1970s and early 1980s, when there were double-digit yields on CDs. So, while money invested in debt instruments means your money is always working, the big worry is it might not be working hard enough to keep up with inflation, or working as hard as it could be.

Then there is pocket cash, and while not an asset class, this is a real holding pot for some. If you keep 100 percent of your money in cash—you know, the stuff you carry around in your pocket, wallet, or handbag and not cash equivalents like CDs, savings accounts, Treasury bills, or money market funds— this loose cash isn't working cash, it's opportunity cash. To only stockpile it means that you're probably either expecting a revolution, planning on leaving your spouse, expecting an emergency, or unsure how to invest it. While I can't help you with the risks and rewards of the first three, this book ought to provide you with some ideas on the latter.

Now that you know more about the three primary asset classes—stocks, bonds, and cash—and that each class has its own set of risks, understand that not all asset classes perform the same under the same market conditions. That's the reason why the word on The Street suggests having money invested in each.

When it comes to selecting stock, bond, and money market mutual funds, how you spread your money out among them will depend upon things such as how long you have to invest and how much risk you'd like to take with your money. How much money you'll make from either has as much, if not more, to do with the time period for which you are invested as it does the funds selected. For instance, in

1997, the average general equity fund was up over 24 percent. That means if you'd invested $1,000 into your average stock fund on December 31, 1996, it would have been worth about 1,240 bucks twelve months later.

In 1998, however, the stock market climbed then fell apart, and as of September 24, 1998, the average general stock fund was losing money, off 3.16 percent thus far that year. So, $1,000 invested on December 31, 1997, would have been worth about $970 roughly nine months later.

As to how to allocate your money, most investment models break down their asset allocation suggestions by investor personality characteristics. For example, in the Fidelity model target asset mix below, used in their Personal Investment Review kit in 1998, the headings are for conservative, balanced, growth, and aggressive growth. Here's who each is targeted at and the asset blend suggested:

- *Conservative.* This is the suggested blend for investors who want capital preservation more than they do long-term growth of capital. The blend is a mixture more heavily weighted toward short-term instruments and bonds than stocks.
  20% domestic stocks
  0% foreign stocks
  50% bonds
  30% short-term instruments
- *Balanced.* A combination of income and capital growth is indicated here. Consider diversifying your investments to seek growth combined with less risk over the long term.
  45% domestic stocks
  5% foreign stocks
  40% bonds
  10% short-term instruments
- *Growth.* For those willing to take on more risk in an attempt to outperform conservative investment over the long term.

60% domestic stocks
10% foreign stocks
25% bonds
5% short-term instruments

- *Aggressive Growth.* For those with longer-range goals wanting to consider a more aggressive portfolio.
70% domestic stocks
15% foreign stocks
15% bonds
0% short-term instruments

Again, there's no one right cookie-cutter asset allocation suggestion for everyone. The best anyone can do is to show you what others are suggesting and allow you to use that information as a guideline for creating your own personal allocation plan.

Question 52
How do I know which asset allocation blend is right for me?

By looking at things such as how long you intend to be invested, what your investment goals are, and how much risk you can take with your money.

If you'd like a rule of thumb to go by, for anyone who has short-term investing goals, say they are investing for their kid's college tuition next year or to have the down payment for a home or new car in a year or two, it's probably best to forgo any stock fund investments. The performance of stocks and stock markets typically runs in cycles varying from a couple of years out to five or six. Consequently, if you're not able to keep your money in a stock fund for at least four, five, or six years, and you can't afford to lose principal on any of the money that you're investing, I'd forget stocks and look at money market mutual funds, individual bonds, and short- or medium-term bond funds instead. Where short-term investment time horizons are concerned, sometimes cash and short-term funds pay off the best.

But do you have 5, 10, 15, 20 years or more to invest? Then stocks historically have held the best dollar promise and the least risk.

While time and performance are important elements to understand when creating an asset allocation plan, what's equally as important is your tolerance for risk-taking. Answering the question, "Am I willing to see the value of my overall portfolio drop 25 percent or more?" will give you a clue as to how you feel about that.

Question 53
Do you ever pick up any personal finance tips from the portfolio managers that you interview?

Occasionally. Below is a story I wrote after interviewing Dan Cantor, portfolio manager of the Stein Roe Growth and Income Fund that was full of personal finance tips.

One of the reasons Cantor likes managing the Growth and Income Fund over the Young Investors Fund is that the Growth and Income Fund is more in tune with his nature. One of the reasons I liked interviewing him was because of all the common sense investing tips he provided. Here's the story:

"That (Young Investors) is a growth fund and this (Growth and Income) is really a more risk-adverse fund," says Cantor. "The growth profiles of many of the stocks in the fund are a little less robust. But, what I get from that is the ability to sleep a little bit better at night."

And therein lie Tips Nos. 1 and 2: Get out of any investments that don't allow you to get a restful night's sleep. After a while, sleep-deprived people aren't likely to make wise financial decisions.

Tip No. 2: If taking big risks isn't your cup of tea, there's nothing wrong with pulling back a little, remembering that less risky investments can make money, too.

Cantor keeps between 50 and 60 stocks in this no-load fund's portfolio. During the previous 12 months, the fund's total return was over 23 percent. That's slightly under the performance of the average growth and income fund—it was up over 25 percent—but then again, Cantor's cash position was high. "I had on average about 13 percent cash during the year," he said.

While most mutual funds keep between 5 and 10 percent of their assets invested in cash, a 13 percent position in that asset class can be a drag on performance, particularly in a raging bull market. Which brings us to Tip No. 3, cash. When the market is soaring ahead, a healthy cash position could pull down your portfolio's overall performance. In flat or down markets, cash can be a big plus to performance.

Not all of the stocks in this fund are large caps. Cantor is a bottom-up stock picker who likes to buy great companies at good prices no matter what their size. So, along with names like Warner Lambert and Philip Morris you'll find less formidable companies such as Ecolab, a cleaning services company, and TJX, a retailer with two store names many are familiar with—TJ Maxx and Marshalls.

Two tips worth noting here are to diversify (Tip 4) and understand why you made an investment in the first place (Tip 5).

Regarding diversification, make sure your fund's assets are diversified and that the investments that make up your own personal portfolio are, too. To learn about a fund's holdings first-hand, read their annual report. To diversify your fund holdings, don't own only one kind of fund type, such as all emerging funds or all growth and income funds. Then, put some thought into why you've invested in a particular stock mutual fund and jot it down. You'll be surprised at how helpful notes like that can be. Especially when you're thinking about selling some fund shares or adding to your position.

Morningstar has given Stein Roe's Growth and Income Fund a 4-star rating and considers the fund to be "below average" in the risk department. Along with that below-average risk have come some consistent returns. Over the last three years, the fund's total returns were as follows; up 25.71 percent in 1997; up 21.81 percent in 1996, and up 30.15 percent in 1995. In 1994, when the S&P 500 was up a mere 1.32 percent, this fund was down 0.14 percent.

Consistency is Tip No. 6. Old Money knows that consistent returns are better than those that zigzag all over the board. Let's hear it for Old Money wisdom.

Question 54
When the market is volatile, any ideas for how to assess my investments?

Start with your stomach. If you're looking for shelter in a market environment that's volatile like the one in 1998 was, and think that there's a Mighty Mouse fund out there that can "save the day," think again. James Zisson, a senior vice president and senior investment management consultant at Salomon Smith Barney in West Palm Beach, Florida, suggests the best thing to do when the market is volatile and you're worried too is to do a "gut check." You know, get a take on how you feel about your investments, looking to see if your risk and reward parameters are in synch with one another.

Zisson said that if, for example, you've got a portfolio with 75 percent of its assets exposed to stocks, and, after a rocky ride in the market, have come to realize that you haven't liked the volatility you've witnessed with three-quarters of your investable assets, then it's time to change things. His suggestion: Slow down to your sleeping point. Doing that would mean making some changes in your asset allocation and finding a point at which your investments are still working for you but you're not worrying about them.

Asset allocation, after all, is the way to minimize market volatility. And having a mutual fund portfolio that includes the basics—equity, fixed-income, and money market funds—divvied up into amounts you can live with, is the best market protector you'll probably ever find.

Question 55
My financial planner is always talking about beta, standard deviation, and a bunch of other stuff I know nothing about. What's he trying to tell me?

He's trying to address some risk issues.

Although there is no way to wipe risk out of the investment world, there are ways to get an idea of how much risk a fund has taken on in its past. Those last three words are the ones to remember here.

Morningstar uses a number of different ways to measure risk in their reports. The meanings of the most popular are as follows:

- *Beta.* A statistical measure that shows how volatile a fund is. It uses the number 1.0 as home base. A fund with a beta higher than 1, for instance, will be a fund that's more volatile than the market. One with a beta of 0.75 will be less volatile than the market.
- *Sector Concentration.* Investing in just one industry sector also takes you to the extreme in fund risk. That's because sectors run hot and cold performance-wise.
- *Stock Concentration.* If your fund invests in only a handful of stocks, it's considered riskier than those funds that invest in many dozen. While technically that is true, through the first half of 1998, some of the best-performing funds were those with concentrated portfolios.
- *Standard Deviation.* This statistical measurement shows how much a fund's investment returns have varied over

a given period of time. The wider the variation or swing, the higher the risk.

Keep in mind, while there is value in looking at what kinds of risk a fund has taken on in the past, and things like beta will give you an idea of how its past performance mirrors that of the markets, use this information as one part of the package of information that you've gathered about a fund. Like a fund's performance figures, these too show what has happened yesterday. And yesterday is no guarantee of what will come tomorrow.

Question 56
What's wrong with buying individual stocks rather than mutual funds? Or buying them as well as investing in funds?

Nothing. Plenty of people have made piles of money investing in individual stocks. Lots of folks also invest in both stocks and funds. The whole idea behind investing is to make money. Any way—or combinations of ways—that you can come up with to do that is great.

The benefits of buying funds are that you're buying professional management, along with diversification and convenience, all at a low cost. Plus, there are no liquidity issues—getting in and out of your fund investments can happen on any business day of the week—which is not always the case in all individual issues of stock.

Just as there are thousands of mutual funds to select from, there are thousands of stocks to pick from, too. Consequently, finding a company that you'd like to invest in will take some time and effort—just as selecting a mutual fund does.

That being said, before making your first stock and/or mutual fund investment, think money first.

You can often get started in mutual fund investing with just a few hundred bucks. Getting into stocks, however, can take more. That dollar cost depends upon the per-share price of the stock, how many shares of it you purchase, and commission fees. With mutual funds, you can cut out sales charges by investing in no-load funds, which have no sales commissions. But when buying individual stocks there is always a fee for buying and selling them, unless you're buying shares of an initial public offering (IPO), and in that case the commission for buying the shares is included in the per-share price of the stock.

A couple of ways to minimize commission costs are to set up on-line accounts—commissions for buying and selling stocks on-line are considerably less than when working through many brokerage firms. Or, buy the stocks directly from the company itself. In that case you'll pay some fees for setting up your account—typically those fees range from $5 to $30—and you can purchase any number of shares from one to whatever. If you'd like to buy stocks directly from a company, two great resources for learning about the firms that offer such plans are The DRIP Investor/No-Load Stock Insider newsletter (1-800-233-5922) and this Web site: www.netstockdirect.com.

In the end, there is nothing wrong with an investment goal that sets out to create a portfolio that contains a few good stocks and mutual funds. Go for it.

Question 57
What about bear market funds and market neutral funds? Aren't they supposed to be the perfect investments for times when the market runs amuck?

Although bear market investment strategies have been around for years, most bear and market neutral funds haven't been around long enough for the pros to see if the investing public will go for them. But, should you like the idea of investing in different types of funds designed to stave off the wolves during market downturns and don't know what your choices are, here's how some fund types weathered last year's market storm:

- *Bear market funds.* In bear market funds, portfolio managers typically bet against the market, selling stocks short and/or investing in inflation-sensitive hard assets that are expected to go up when the market goes down. Lipper Analytical Services, Inc. tracks eight bear market funds. The top performing ones from June 18, 1998 through September 17, 1998, were the Prudent Bear Fund, up 14.94 percent, and the Profounds: Ultrabear Investors fund, ahead 13.769 percent for the same time period. Year-to-date performance numbers showed both funds down more than 8 percent.
- *Market neutral funds.* Here, portfolios typically hold stocks in both positions—long and short. (A long position means that you own the stocks outright. In short positions you don't—stocks are borrowed.) For a market

neutral fund to be a winner in a down market, the portfolio manager has to have picked the right stocks to short, and the short portfolio gains have to go up in value faster and greater than those held as long positions. In an up market, to come out ahead the opposite needs to be true. The Barr Rosen: Market Neutral Investors fund was up 1.90 percent for that same time period, while The Euclid Market Neutral fund was down 1.14 percent.

- *Utility funds.* Although the group as a whole was down 4.48 percent for the third quarter of 1998, it was the best-performing fund type in the fourth quarter of 1997. The top-performing utility fund in mid-September 1998 was the Morgan Stanley Dean Witter Global Utility fund. It was up 17.73 percent year-to-date and down 2.50 percent for the first 13 weeks in the third quarter. Icon's Telecommunications & Utility fund held the No. 1 spot for that 13-week period, as it was ahead 1.86 percent. For the year, it had gained 12.21 percent.

- *Gold funds.* Most people don't know what to make of gold funds because they have been pretty horrible investments over the past 10 years. Bad investment or not, however, plenty of people still believe in gold. The top-performing gold fund through mid-September 1998—and thus far that year—was the Lexington Strategic Investors Gold fund. It was up 4.55 percent in the quarter, and down 5.74 percent for the year.

If you'd like to invest in any of these fund types, with the exception of utility funds, don't plan on investing much. Allocating about 5 percent of your total assets into gold, market neutral, or bear market funds is the typical suggestion.

Question 58
I'd like to invest in emerging markets funds. Is that a good idea?

Emerging markets funds hold a lot of sex appeal. They provide folks with an investment entrée in exotic markets in faraway places from Singapore to St. Petersburg to Rio—spots most people probably will never visit and only read about. As profit potential, these markets look enticing. But, in the last five years, they haven't done so well.

Numbers from Lipper ending September 30, 1998 show that all Pacific-ex Japan funds (excluding Japan funds), Japanese funds, Pacific region funds, China region funds, Latin American funds, Canadian funds, and Emerging Markets funds have lost money for their investors over the last five years. The biggest losses for this year have been Latin American funds (down over 42 percent), Emerging Markets funds (off well over 35 percent), and China region funds (down nearly 32 percent), from December 31, 1997 through September 30, 1998.

Because people hate losing money, I consider emerging markets funds to be very risky investments. And, if I were to invest in an emerging markets fund, find it performing handsomely for a year or so, I'd be inclined to take those profits. Why? Because on balance, emerging markets are too new, too unregulated, and their governments often too unfamiliar with the ins and outs of operating in a free-market environment to provide investors with any stable long-term results. Examples of these facts came to light in 1997 and 1998.

As one portfolio manager put it, "August [1998] was a hideous month for emerging markets." And he was right.

But what about the future? Isn't there plenty of money to be made in emerging markets? Yes, there probably is. But, the question that you, an investor, have to answer isn't whether or not there is money to be made, but whether or not you want to take the risk of investing capital in an emerging markets fund. If your answer is yes, most pros say that someone's portfolio ought to include an international component representing somewhere between 5 and 25 percent of their total assets. If you decide to allocate a portion of your money in that fashion, then the next questions are: Where in the world do I want to invest? Do I want to invest in emerging markets? and, finally, Which emerging markets?

In the end, emerging markets are a play for those who a) know what they are getting into; b) have a stomach for big-time market volatility; and c) know better than to allocate a lot of money to the various regions—5 percent of one's assets is often enough.

Question 59
How many funds do I need
to own?

A couple is often enough to get the job done.

I met a man a few years ago who owned over 40 different mutual funds. An enthusiast about buying funds, he had a hard time ever parting with any.

Basically, I think two or three funds is enough to get started and create a diversified portfolio of funds. My suggestions for those two funds would be a money market mutual fund and an index fund. Preferably an S&P 500 index fund. If I wanted to add a third fund, it would be a global or international fund.

The money market fund is a great place to park money, keep your savings and rainy day money, use as a source for some of your long-term investing dollars and a fixed-income safe haven for your buckeroos. The S&P 500 index fund represents an equity investment that's inexpensive to maintain, invests in large, established companies, and historically performs better than the vast majority of equity funds.
Together, those two types of funds can carry you a long way.

Add a global or international component in which the long-term performance records are hard to beat, and you've got a portfolio that's not only well-diversified but circles the globe.

And that's the short answer to the question. The longer one is, I know financial planners that ask their clients to invest into a couple of handfuls of funds just so that they'll have a diversified portfolio. In this case the lineup often includes a money market mutual fund; an index fund; a global and/or international fund; some type of growth fund; micro-, small-, medium-, or large-cap fund; a value fund; a balanced fund; an income fund; a specialty sector fund; and an emerging markets fund.

That's an awful lot of funds to keep track of, and can cause one to slip into that dreaded investing disease called "fund buildup"—something that can happen without your even knowing it. If you've got an IRA that you contribute to each year and invest in different funds every couple of years, a 401(k), SEP–IRA, or Keogh account that you also contribute to annually and occasionally fund differently, and a personal portfolio made up of various funds, you can wind up with dozens of fund investments without even trying. Hence the term, fund buildup.

While there is nothing wrong with owning lots of funds, beware of owning funds if

- you don't know their names,
- you can't remember why you invested in them,
- they overlap one another in investment strategies, asset types, and portfolio holdings, or
- they haven't performed well for you.

My suggestion for how many funds to own is as simple as one, two, three:

1. Only own mutual funds that you know the full name of.
2. Only own funds in which you understand where the fund invests its money, believe in the types of investments it makes, and understand its investment strategy.
3. And, only own funds that make money. That means on the fixed income side, if you can only own one fund, let that one be a money market mutual fund. Like revved-up savings accounts, money market mutual funds are designed to provide you with a yield on your investment dollars and one that's higher than those on passbook savings accounts. So, if you've got a savings

account, moving some or all of the money from it into a money market account will allow your money to work harder for you.

From money market mutual funds, newcomers might want to eventually tiptoe into stock funds. For the least risky ones, consider blue-chip stock funds, large-cap stock funds, international and global, and balanced or flexible funds. Aggressive fund investors would seek out micro- or small-cap funds, specialty funds, and emerging markets funds.

Even though there is never any guarantee that a stock fund will make you any money, to follow the "only own funds that make you money" rule, before you invest, find out the benchmark that your fund selection is measured against, and then don't buy a fund whose past performance doesn't at least equal if not outperform that benchmark over selected time periods. That way, you'll be buying the best funds—ones that have made people money in the past.

Speaking of the past, again, a fund's past performance is no indication of how that fund will perform in the future. But it is an indication of how the fund has performed over its lifetime, under various market conditions and fund managers. So, while a fund's past performance history offers no future performance promises, it does provide some groundwork from which the fund selection process can then begin.

In the final analysis, two or three selectively chosen diversified funds can be enough to get the job done. So can six to ten. But get over a dozen funds and if the paperwork won't drive you crazy, trying to figure out what the funds really invest in might.

Question 60
What's the big to-do about
international investing?

Thanks to cables and satellites, the world is a much smaller place today than it was 20 years ago. Because it's smaller, the opportunity for investing around the globe has increased dramatically.

One of the most recognized people to see that there were investment opportunities outside of the United States was Sir John Templeton. Templeton was one of the pioneers who decades ago turned investors on to international investing via mutual funds. And since his move, dozens of fund families have created funds that invest in companies all around the world.

Like everything else in the fund industry, the push for international investing all boils down to money. And, in every corner of the world there is money to be made. Twenty-five years ago roughly 65 percent of the world's publicly traded stocks were made up of U.S. company stocks. In early 1998 that figure had dwindled to 43 percent. The figures on page 129 show where some of the top world markets have been and their share of the world's equity market.

As far as performance goes, U.S. and world markets don't generally perform in tandem. Because of that, adding an international or global component to your portfolio adds diversification.

Top-performing developed markets	% of world's equity share
1995	
Switzerland	42%
U.S.	34%
Sweden	33%
1996	
Finland	37%
Hong Kong	35%
Sweden	35%
1997	
Switzerland	46%
Spain	41%
Italy	37%

Source: Founder's Funds/Bloomberg

Question 61
How far will investing just a few dollars a month—like $25 to $100—in a mutual fund get me?

No one can guarantee the results you'll get—that all depends upon the fund(s) you've selected, how well it's managed, and market conditions during the time of fund ownership. But, going strictly by the numbers, a little bit of money can go an awfully long way.

There are dozens of mutual funds that allow investors to start investing with $25, $50, or $100 a month. The trick to making money investing the same amounts of money is consistently. Money methodically has to be invested month-after-month and year-after-year to reap any substantial rewards, with the size of the investment as much as you want but no less than the fund's minimal investment requirement. (You'll find out how much that is in the fund's prospectus.)

So if you don't have hundreds—or thousands—of dollars to invest, even $25 a month can grow into tens of thousands of dollars, depending upon the length of time it is invested and its annual rate of return.

To show how consistency pays off, in July 1997 I asked CDA/Wiesenberger, the Rockland, Maryland-based mutual fund research company, to run some numbers. Here are the parameters for the research:

- The average annual rates of return chosen were 8, 10, and 14 percent.

- The time periods selected included 1, 5, 10, 20, and 30 years.
- Monthly contributions ranged from $25 to $50 to $100.
- And, no taxes were figured into these calculations.

Now the results:

$25 a month invested in an account earning 8 percent a year will grow to

$311 at the end of one year;
$1,837 at the end of 5 years;
$4,573 at the end of 10 years;
$14,725 at the end of 20 years;
$37,259 at the end of 30 years.

If that $25 were compounding at a tax-deferred annual rate of 10 percent, its value would be

$314 in one year;
in 5 years, $1,936;
in 10 years, $5,121;
in 20 years, $18,984;
and in 30 years, $56,512.

Bump the annual rate of return up to an average of 14 percent and a monthly investment of $25 grows to

$2,155 in 5 years;
$32,529 in 20 years;
and a whopping $137,324 in 30 years.

If a $50 monthly investment is within your reach, you would have

$3,674 in 5 years;
$9,147 in 10 years;
$29,451 in 20 years;
and $74,518 in 30 years, if that money was compounding at an average annual rate of 8 percent.

Keep adding $50 a month into an account compounding at 10 percent annually and you'll have

$37,968 in 20 years
and $113,024 at the end of 30 years.

And, if that money ($50 per month) were compounding
at 14 percent a year,
in 5 years you'd have $4,310;
in 10 years, $12,953;
in 20 years, $65,058;
and in 30 years, an impressive $274,648.

For those with $100 a month to invest regularly, an 8
percent return would grow to
$7,348 in 5 years;
$18,295 in 10 years;
$58,902 in 20 years;
and $149,036 in 30 years.

Earning 10 percent annually, monthly payments of $100
would grow to
$20,485 in 10 years;
$75,937 in 20 years;
and $226,049 in 30 years.

And, if you're lucky enough to have money invested in
a fund that returns an average of 14 percent over time,
$100 a month will grow to $1,280 in one year;
$25,907 in 10 years;
$300,117 in 20 years;
and a handsome $549,297 in 30 years.

As you can see, consistency, time, compounding, and
deferring taxes until a later date can actually pay for those
building nest eggs.

Also, note that the really big returns on your money
don't appear until money has been working for about 20
years. Knowing that before you make your first fund investment will help to keep your investment expectations in line.

Question 62
My investment advisor wants me to invest in a variety of different-sized companies. What's the point?

There are lots of reasons to hold small-, medium-, and large-cap funds, but the primary one is performance.

Like everything else in life, stock market prices run in cycles. Consequently, sometimes large-cap funds are in favor, other times it's the small- or mid-sized companies racking up the biggest scores.

For the past few years large capitalized companies, as reflected by the performance of the S&P 500, have been the cycle winners. In the early 1990s, small-cap stocks, as measured by the Russell 2000, outperformed the Big Boys. While no one is certain today what size companies will lead the pack a year from now, many pros say it's more important to be invested across the board—in micro-, small-, medium-, and large-sized companies—rather than try to figure out what cycle the market is in. Why? Because throughout history, small-, medium-, and large-cap funds have all had their heydays and performed well.

For instance, in 1991, large-cap stocks moved ahead 28 percent and small-caps, over 38 percent. In 1992, small-cap stocks returned over twice what the large-caps did, 16.3 percent and 7.6 percent, respectively. In 1993, the score was small-caps ahead 16.2 percent; large-caps up 9.8 percent. But by year-end 1994, things had started to change: Small-caps were down 2.7 percent while the large-caps moved ahead almost 2 percent, according to Lipper Analytical Services.

Since 1995, the road has been a solid one for larger-sized corporations. In 1995, the large-caps gained over 32 percent, 8 percent more than stocks in the Russell 2000. In 1996, small-caps were up almost 15 percent and the S&P 500 gained over 21 percent. By year-end 1997, the average small-cap fund was up over 20 percent; the average mid-cap fund ahead by well over 19 percent; and the large-caps, as represented by the S&P 500 funds, had well over 32 percent.

By the end of June 1998, things were beginning to change: Although the large-cap stock funds were still the big winners, the performance of mid-cap funds had moved out in front of small-cap funds.

Porter Morgan, Liberty Financial Companies investment strategist, says that market cycles typically will last from two to five years. But, like performance numbers, the best way to read investment cycles is historically. So the best way to catch a market-cycle trend is to always be invested in large-cap as well as medium- and small-cap companies.

If you'd like to have your assets spread among various-sized companies, there are a couple of ways to do that. One is to invest in funds that only place their assets into small, medium, or large companies. Another is to invest in funds that invest in a variety of different-sized companies—you'll find that information out from the fund's prospectus, from its annual report, or by asking a fund sales rep or your investment advisor.

But small, medium, and large aren't the only three company sizes that funds can be classified in. The latest capitalization category in Lipper's performance universe is micro-cap funds. Funds that fall under this category are the smallest companies—those with market capitalizations less than $300 million at the time of purchase. By June 30, 1998, there were 53 such funds in Lipper's universe.

Question 63
I've heard that funds new to the market outperform established ones. Any truth to that?

For years, those in the know have been telling fund investors to only investigate mutual funds that have established track records. Now, studies show that brand-new equity funds outperform their peers—in the beginning, anyway.

In early 1998, the Kobren Insight Group, a Wellesley Hills, Massachusetts-based money management and financial newsletter publisher, conducted a study that showed "overall, domestic equity mutual funds perform better during their rookie year" than other funds in like categories. While the level of performance varied among fund types, in general, this study's findings indicated that the average new large- and mid-cap funds outperformed their peers by 2.1 percentage points in their first year of existence. Small-cap funds did even better. They outperformed their peers by 6.9 percent. Look at small-cap growth funds and the performance ball gets hit way out of the park; they outperformed their peer group by 9.2 percent during their first 12 months on the market.

The Schwab Center for Investment Research also published a report on the same subject that year. Their findings were similar, showing that "new domestic equity funds have had higher returns than their older peers fairly consistently during recent years."

Looking into the whys behind the better performance, the Schwab report said that the higher returns were driven by greater risk-taking on the part of the new fund. And, "on a risk-adjusted return basis, only new small-company growth funds have outperformed their older peers."

To the investor having a hard time trying to decide which fund to purchase shares of, study results like this could lead one to believe that picking a fund is easy—just go with the newest on the market. But, like every investment strategy, things aren't ever as simple as they sound.

If you'd like to try your hand at investing in new funds and don't mind taking on the risk, trying to get on top of what fund family is bringing out a new fund and when is probably the biggest hurdle you'll have to cross. One reason for that is because there is no single source dedicated to listing new funds that's easily accessible to the individual investor. Even those familiar with using the SEC's on-line site (sec.com.) are likely to find that resource frustrating unless they are familiar with all aspects of it.

Sources that offer new fund-listing information to investors include newsletter publications—like the *Morningstar Investor*—and the fund families themselves. Fund families always send out press releases about their new funds to all major print, news, and media sources. Unfortunately, most new fund notices wind up in the wastepaper basket. Fund families also notify their existing shareholders of the new funds they are introducing, and that's probably the best way to learn about them.

If you've been able to gather the prospectus and all the info you need about a new fund, buying it just because it's new isn't particularly wise. Smarter reasons to invest would include because you like the fund manager and his or her investing style or philosophy, and you want to invest in the area of the market the fund invests its assets into.

Finally, remember these studies show only one-year performance numbers. Currently there is no long-term data supporting any high-performance return consistencies.

Question 64
When is the best time to invest my money in a fund that invests in the S&P 500 or in stocks that are a part of that index?

Lots of people will tell you that the best time to invest is "when you've got the money." Others will say "anytime." Since there is no one absolute answer to that question, just for the fun of it, here's a hypothetical look at how money changes value when invested in the S&P 500, on the "best" and "worst" days of the market.

The John Hancock Funds family summoned TowersData, a research company that creates financial hypothetical data, to create two charts—one showing how an investment in the S&P 500 index would fare over the last 10 years if $10,000 were invested each year on the one day of the year that the S&P 500 were at its annual high and left to accumulate over time, the other showing how money would grow if invested on the one day of the year that index hit its low. (Taxes were not a part of either calculation.)

The results of these "best" and "worst" investment day scenarios are as follows:

- If you had invested $10,000 at the worst time every year, the one day in the year that the market hit its high, here's how your investment track record would read:

Market High	Cumulative Invested	Year-end Account Value
Oct 21, 1988	$10,000	$9,878
Oct 9, 1989	$20,000	$22,900
Jul 16, 1990	$30,000	$31,310
Dec 31, 1991	$40,000	$50,808
Dec 18, 1992	$50,000	$64,616
Dec 28, 1993	$60,000	$81,070
Feb 2, 1994	$70,000	$91,980
Dec 13, 1995	$80,000	$136,386
Nov 25, 1996	$90,000	$177,453
Dec 5, 1997	$100,000	Total value: $246,476

Even investing on these "worst" days, the average annual total return for this 10-year time period is 18.20 percent.

- If you had invested $10,000 at the "best" time every year, the one day in the year that the market hit its low, here's how your investment track record would read:

Market Low	Cumulative Invested	Year-end Account Value
Jan 20, 1988	$10,000	$11,863
Jan 3, 1989	$20,000	$28,885
Oct 11, 1990	$30,000	$39,267
Jan 9, 1991	$40,000	$64,997
Apr 8, 1992	$50,000	$81,237
Jan 8, 1993	$60,000	$100,563
Apr 4, 1994	$70,000	$112,624
Mar 1, 1995	$80,000	$168,546
Jan 10, 1996	$90,000	$219,791
Jan 2, 1997	$100,000	Total value: $306,414

Investing on the "best" days, money worked at an average annual return rate of 20.22 percent.

Although past performance numbers are no indication of how the markets will perform in the future, hypotheticals like this illustrate—among other things—that during extended bull markets, even bad days can look good at any given time.

Bad Days

Up and down movements in the stock market are natural and to be expected. So, while few measure, or complain, about the percentage gains when the market is rising, when it starts to fall each percentage movement downward is an event.
Here are some of the biggest declines in this century.

The Ten Worst Stock Market Declines Since 1926

Year	Decline in S&P 500 Index
1931	-43.3%
1937	-35.0%
1974	-26.5%
1930	-24.9%
1973	-14.7%
1941	-11.6%
1957	-10.8%
1966	-10.1%
1940	-9.8%
1962	-8.7%

Source: ICI

Question 65
You've shown me a hypothetical about how the S&P 500 has performed in recent markets. Can you show me how the numbers would look if the time frame was from 1970 to 1980—when bear and flat markets were the norm?

Good question.

TowersData, the same Bethesda, Maryland company that provided the numbers for Question 64 has run the numbers from 1970 to 1980, as you suggested.

Keep in mind that the S&P 500 went from 120.24 on January 1, 1973 to 62.28 on October 3, 1974. So, as you might guess, the results aren't as compelling. But they aren't horrible, either.

Assuming that you had invested $10,000 faithfully, every year during the decade of the 1970s on the one day of the year that the S&P 500 hit its high point, reinvested all dividends and capital gains, and had no tax consequences to pay on this investment, your total investment of $100,000 would have grown in value to $129,689. That works out to an average annual total return of 5.01 percent.

Looking at the carnage during the worst years of that decade—between year-end 1972 and year-end 1974—the total value of your investment changed as follows:

- On December 31, 1972, a $30,000 investment was worth $35,749;
- one year later in 1973, $40,000 was worth $38,883; and
- at year-end 1974, $50,000 worth $35,856.

It took until year's end in 1975 for the tide to begin to turn: Then, your $60,000 investment had a value of $58,809. One year later, the investment of $70,000 was worth $82,978. And from then on, each year this investment continued to make money.

But, if you were lucky enough to have picked the one day each year in which the S&P 500 had hit its low point, that $100,000 investment would have blossomed to $165,916. Money in this case would have been working for you at an average annual total return rate of 9.75 percent. As for the ugly years, here's what happened:

- At year-end 1972, $30,000 was worth $44,111;
- one year later, $40,000 was worth $48,329; and
- at year-end 1974, a $50,000 investment was worth $46,776.

Make-believe investors in this scenario didn't have to wait as long to recoup their losses and have their money grow. Things changed for them by year-end 1975, when their $60,000 investment had a value of $77,574.

The moral to this story is twofold:

- On the one hand, research continues to show that long-term investing can pay off even through bear and flat markets, provided investors are willing to hang on as the market fluctuates.
- On the other hand, timing does play a big part in the kinds of returns that the market doles out.

Question 66
What is market timing?
And why does everyone
seem to discourage it?

Marketing timing is an investment strategy that banks on you knowing precisely when the market is going to change course.

For instance, savvy market timers probably would have sold all of their big-cap stock funds before the middle of July 1998, never have invested in small-cap funds for the past couple of years, and definitely would have gotten out of emerging markets, Asian, or Latin American funds a few years back. To be an effective market timer you've got to be able to see into the future and know what it's going to bring so that you can protect your capital by not getting caught in any market downturns. By the same token, you've also got to be able to know when things are going to turn around again so that you'll be able to accurately take advantage of any fresh upside gains.

According to Ibbotson Research, if you missed being in the market during the 15 months that stocks scored their biggest advances during the last two decades, you would have given up 76% of the gains the market made. Figures from Fidelity show that $1,000 invested in the S&P 500 in 1978 was worth $21,750 in 1998 (calculations were figured through March 1998). Missing those 15 months, however, brings that return down drastically—to $6,010.

The reason the strategy is discouraged is that—for most—it doesn't work.

Question 67
Can you recommend a mutual fund for a woman, age 25, who's new to investing? She's got $600 and will be investing for the long term. Is it better to save up $1,000 first?

Gender really has nothing to do with the mutual fund you select. So, the question that needs answering is, what type of fund should a new investor with a long-term investment horizon and 600 bucks to spend think about investing in?

Until that person is able to do some research on her own, to learn about the various types of funds out there and what to expect from them, the first thing I'd do is put that $600 into a money market mutual fund. That way the money will be working for her, at a very competitive rate, until she decides where to move it.

Then, if she's into performance, it's hard to top the long-term historic rates of returns that index funds have offered. Getting into them typically takes from $1,000 to $3,000.

If she likes other types of funds, opening an account with $500 is often very doable. And, adding to that amount on a regular basis is pretty smart. Not only will that get her into the investing habit, a great habit to have, it could pay off handsomely in the long run, too.

So, the money market mutual fund will get her started, show her how money can grow, and provide her with the lowest-risk fund out there. The next move from there depends upon her preferences. Those will take time for her to figure out.

Question 68

I've recently retired and plan to roll over my lump sum pension benefits into a taxable fixed-income mutual fund. I want to minimize principal risk and maximize my return. I have concerns over a further reduction in interest rates and how it might impact bond funds. Do you have any advice or guidance?

Choices of bond funds include those considered the very safest—they would be those that only invest in government-backed securities, like Treasury bonds or government agency ones, considered safest because most assume that the government will make timely interest and principal payments on the debts it issues—to corporate bond funds, which run the gamut from AAA rated to non-rated high-yielding funds. Any change in interest rates means a change in bond prices and their returns.

Your concern over a further reduction in interest rates is a good point. If you remember back to the early 1980s when bonds had coupon yields of 12-plus percent, as interest rates fell the total return on bond funds went up. As a result, the historical long-term performance numbers on many bond funds has been pretty attractive. But that's looking backward. Going forward things might not be the same.

Today, with yields on long-term, high-quality bonds under 6 percent, things are different. And, because it's a far bigger fall from 12 to 6 percent than it is from 6 to, say, 5 or 4 percent, it's unlikely that bond funds will rack up the same handsome long-term total returns in the near future as they have in the past.

What this all means is, if you are looking to invest in a bond fund for its total return, expect its return to fluctuate as interest rates do. And, invest in the highest-quality bond funds made up of bonds maturing in the short- to medium-term to minimize principal risk. Investors can pick up most of a bond's yield and take on less of its investment risk by investing in bonds that mature in the mid-term.

Question 69
Do bond funds make sense in a bull market?

That all depends upon what your goals and needs are.

Many investment professionals will tell you that it's best to have your money invested across the board in all three asset classes—stocks, bonds, and cash—at all times no matter what asset class is sitting in the bull's seat. How much in each depends upon things like how aggressive you are with your investing monies, your investment goals, and what your immediate needs for that cash are. Professional opinions aside, I know people who don't care for the stock market no matter how wonderful conditions in it are. For them, bonds and any other kind of fixed-income product—like CDs—are the only way to go. As always, it's personal preference that usually dictates how you invest, no matter what market conditions prevail.

To build a case for owning fixed-income funds when stocks are hot, let's look at the performance figures for both stock and long-term bond funds over the last couple of years. (A long-term bond fund includes everything *but* a money market fund.)

By year-end 1996, the average stock fund had gained nearly 19.5 percent; general bond funds gained about 6 percent. From January 1 through May 5, 1997, the total return for the average bond fund moved up less than 1 percent, while the average stock fund gained more than 4 percent. At year-end 1997 the score was general equity funds up 24.26 percent, long-term fixed income funds ahead 10.26 percent. Midway through 1998, the average general equity fund was up 11.75 percent, and the general long-term domestic taxable fixed-income fund had gained only 1.43 percent, according to Lipper Analytical Services.

One look at the numbers shows two things: First and foremost, both stock and bond fund returns bounce around. So don't expect one to necessarily provide you with a more stable return than the other. And second, when stocks are shooting upwards, it's easy to forget bonds if you're only looking at performance numbers. Bond pros, however, will tell you to look at things like real returns—that's a figure that's arrived at when taking the yield on a long-term Treasury and subtracting the current rate of inflation from it. The result is called a "real rate" of return. Under mid-1998 market conditions, with long-term rates below 6 percent and inflation less than 2 percent, a 4 percent real rate of return from a fixed-income investment historically isn't such a bad deal.

On another front, Franklin Templeton research shows that bonds can be less volatile investments than stocks. For instance, between January 1, 1973 and December 31, 1996, in their worst performance year, bonds were down minus 4 percent. In their best year, they gained 31 percent. As for stocks, when they sank the most during that time frame they fell over 26 percent. When they rose, the most they were up was 38 percent. Over the long haul, the average annual return on stocks between 1973 and 1996 was 12.30 percent. For bonds, it was 9.05 percent.

In the end, no matter what the pros say, people often invest with their stomachs—those who can't handle the gyrations of the stock market, and need a fixed income stream, typically wind up having a greater portion—or all—of their monies invested in bonds or bond funds. Those who are looking for their assets to grow opt for more—or all—stocks.

One further point: Prices on all stocks, need you be reminded one more time, don't always go up. John Kallis, a senior vice president at State Street Research and portfolio manager of the State Street Research Immediate Fund and the Strategic Income Fund, points out that if corporate earnings don't continue to grow, it's hard to continually make money in stocks.

"Owning only stocks is fine and well and good as long as earnings continue to expand. But if corporations start to get their margins squeezed and they can't raise prices, their costs go up, their margins go down, and companies aren't going to earn the kinds of rates they've been earning," says Kallis. "So, if anyone is uncomfortable with the multiples on stocks, the bond market is the place to be."

Question 70
Is there any way to get more zing out of an index fund?

Yep—look for an actively managed one or an enhanced index portfolio.

Index funds—funds designed to mirror the performance of an index (the most popular being S&P 500 index funds)—have become wildly popular over the last few years. At the end of 1995, for instance, there were only 44 of them around, according to Lipper Analytical Services. By mid-year 1998, there were 94.

While the vast majority of these funds are unmanaged—or passively managed—there is another side developing. It is referred to as actively managed index funds.

An actively managed index fund is one whose portfolio manager actively uses investment strategies that he or she hopes will ratchet the fund's performance ahead of that of the index the fund is benchmarked to. Passively managed index funds don't employ those strategies. Computer-driven programs decide how to invest the fund's assets in the same securities—with the same industry and sector weightings—as the index that they follow does.

The goal of the actively managed index fund is to add value and outperform the specific index the fund tracks. But not by much—say 30 to 150 basis points. (A basis point is the term used in quoting yields. One hundred basis points is equivalent to 1 percent. Fifty basis points is written as 0.50 and is equal to ½ of 1 percent.)

Many money pros today consider index funds to be a core investment product for their clients whether they select passively or actively managed ones. That's because of their strong performance history and low annual expense ratios. Oh, and don't forget, even though the upside potential of active or unmanaged index funds sounds great, remember that flat and down markets happen, too. When those markets roll around, expect your index fund—no matter how it's managed—to pretty much perform similarly to the index it is designed to follow.

Question 71
I'd like to invest in no-load funds but don't have much money. Are there any no-loads I can get into on the cheap?

Sure. But not as many as there used to be.

When I first started writing about mutual funds in 1988, there were dozens and dozens of funds around that had minimum initial investment requirements ranging between 25 and 500 bucks. Today, that's all changed, and most load and no-load funds are asking for bigger commitments from folks interested in fund investing.

Here's a list of 10 pure no-load stock funds ("pure no-load" meaning that each has no load, and redemption fees or 12 b-1 fees less than 0.25 percent) that Morningstar came up with in February 1998. Initial minimum investment requirement on each is $250 or less. Listed in alphabetical order they were:

- *Adams Equity*, a mid-cap value fund with no minimum investment requirements. That means accounts can be opened with $1 if you so desire.
- *Amana Growth*, a large value fund that invests based on Islamic religious principles. Minimum investment is $100.
- *Amana Income*, a large value fund, invests based on Islamic principles. Minimum investments here are also $100.
- *Armstrong Associates*, a large-cap growth fund, has a minimum initial investment of $250.

- *Leonetti Balanced* is categorized as a domestic hybrid fund. It takes $100 to begin investing in it.
- *MSB Fund.* This long-term capital appreciation fund has a minimum initial investment of $50.
- *Muhlenkamp,* a mid-cap value fund with an initial minimum requirement of $200.
- *Stonebridge Growth* is a large blend growth fund with a $250 initial minimum investment requirement.
- *Strong Asset Allocation,* a domestic hybrid fund, asks only $250 from folks who want to be shareholders in it.
- *Strong Total Return,* a large growth fund with a $250 initial minimum investment.

Look further and you'll often find that many of the stock or bond funds in one family of funds have the same initial minimum investment requirements. So don't let this list of 10 make you think that that's all the funds out there with low minimum investment requirements. It's not. There are many.

Low initial investments, however, are becoming dinosaurs in the fund industry. But there is one exception—the amount it takes to open qualified retirement accounts such as an IRA or 401(k). When retirement is at stake, fund families make it very inexpensive for investors to open accounts.

As always, it pays to shop around. But don't let the opening ante be your only criterion in choosing a fund. Performance is the primary reason for investing. So if you've got to save up in order to open an account with the fund family of your choice, it might be worth it.

Question 72
How do I know when to sell my fund shares?

When you need the money, your goals are met, or you're losing sleep.

Deciding when to sell your fund shares can be as nerve-racking an experience as trying to decide which fund(s) to invest in.

A friend of mine wanted to sell some of one of her fund's shares in May 1998. That was when the stock market was still flying high and it looked as though the bulls would never lose control. So, while she wanted to sell, she felt like she was bucking the trend.

"I invested the money to help pay for my daughter's college education," says this mother of two. "Now I've already made more than I expected. And, since I know that I'll need the money in the fall, I figured I'd sell now just to make sure the money is there."

While the whisper of the word "sell" in the stock market seems almost anti-American, the reality is, the reason most people buy mutual fund shares in the first place is to sell them at some later date—hopefully, after they have made a profit on the investment.

Getting advice about when to redeem some or all of your fund shares, however, can be tricky. That's because there are so many different sides to the subject. Ask a portfolio manager, who gets paid for picking stocks and making money, when to sell and most of them will tell you it's when they've found a better investment. Investing, you see, isn't a long-term deal for them, it's an ongoing thing.

Harold Ireland, portfolio manager of Evergreen Aggressive Growth Fund, said that investors pay him to buy the best investments all the time, no matter if the market is high or low, fully valued or reasonably valued. Buying the best investments he can is what his job is all about.

Since most of us aren't portfolio managers, "long-term" usually has some date—or goal—affixed to it; staying in a fund is not an ad infinitum kind of thing, unless our goal has been to invest in a fund that we intend to pass on to our heirs.

Before the bull market of the 1980s and '90s caught on fire, it seemed that people used to invest more strategically. For instance, when I was a broker in the early 1980s, my clients would invest, and then, when they'd made something like 20 or 30 percent on their money, they'd sell, take their profits, deal with the taxes, and make another investment. That strategy worked well then, and it still does today—especially for those buying individual stocks. As for mutual funds, in those days, most had front-end loads of 8.5 percent. So, to make any money from them meant working off that load. And that took time—as in years.

Now, money has seemed easy to make in the markets. And as long as that remains the case, it's really hard to give advice on when to sell your investments—other than when you need the money and/or your goals have been met.

What I suggest is, before you invest, make sure you've got a Big Picture investment strategy in place. Not only will that provide you with clues on when to sell, but it will keep you focused on why you invested in the first place.

Part 5
Particulars

The devil is always in the details. So you say you don't know how to open a mutual fund account, or you want to open an account for your kids, or maybe you want to invest in mutual funds on-line? You'll find out how to do all of these things—and more—in Part 5.

Question 73
Once I decide to buy shares of a mutual fund, what's involved in opening an account?

There are a few steps involved in opening a mutual fund account. While none of them are difficult or tricky, all are very important. That's because the way your account is registered dictates all sorts of things from who can buy and sell shares of the fund, to who gets the checks and who is responsible for paying the taxes assessed because of this investment.

The first thing to do before opening a fund account is acquire an account application form. You'll find one in either the fund's prospectus, Profile prospectus, the packet of material the fund family sends to you, or your broker/financial advisor will have one. Then comes filling in the blanks.

For anyone opening a regular account, as opposed to a retirement account, some of the questions asked include whose name the fund account is to be registered in, this person's address, phone, and Social Security numbers, and whether you want the dividends and capital gains the fund may kick off either reinvested back into the account or sent directly to you.

On retirement accounts, additional questions include the type of account you're opening, i.e., IRA, Roth IRA, SEP-IRA, etc., if the account is a transfer or rollover, and who the beneficiary will be.

Here's a look at the various ways in which you can open a mutual fund account and have the fund shares registered:

- *Individual accounts or sole ownership.* A mutual fund account opened in one person's name means that that person bears the responsibility for all tax consequences—including reporting and paying tax tariffs—of that investment and is the only one authorized to decide when to buy, sell, or trade fund shares.
- *Joint ownership.* There are several ways to register and own property jointly. One is by registering an account as Joint Tenants With Rights Of Survivorship (JTWROS). Another is Tenancy by the Entirety—that's for husbands and wives only. A third is Tenancy in Common. And a fourth is Community Property. Here's a look at each:
  - *Joint Tenancy With Rights Of Survivorship (JTWROS)* is a popular way for two—or more—individuals to register an account in both names. While the people named on the account don't have to be married or even related, the reason folks tend to like this form of registration is because it meets a need—when an owner dies, ownership of the fund automatically goes to the other name(s) listed on the account, thus avoiding probate.

    There is no limit to the number of names you can have registered as JTWROS, but be careful not to get too carried away here. A fund registered with a whole roster of names can cause problems when it comes to making any account changes, like deciding when to sell fund shares or who can cash the checks the fund kicks off.

    According to the pros at T. Rowe Price, the checks sent out to their shareholders always have all the names on them as they appear on the fund account. So, if lots of names are registered on the account, it will take rounding up all those folks and having them sign the check before it can be cashed.
  - *Tenants in Common.* This sounds a lot like a JTWROS account, but is not. In a JTWROS, 100 percent of the fund's ownership is shared. But in an account titled

Tenancy in Common, each shareholder owns a specific portion of the fund and may sell or transfer his or her shares without the permission of the other co-owner.

- *Tenancy by the Entirety.* This type of account registration is only available to husbands and wives. Making any changes in accounts registered like this takes two—one can't act without the agreement of the other.
- *Community Property.* Accounts registered as Community Property are just for husbands and wives and are only available in the following nine states: Arizona, California, Idaho, Louisiana, Nevada, New Mexico, Texas, Washington, and Wisconsin.

  Each spouse owns a divisible one-half interest in mutual fund accounts registered like this. When either dies, the survivor takes half and the remaining half is probated and taxable.
- *Trust Under Agreement.* Mutual fund investments can be registered as part of a trust, too. Whether the funds are part of a living trust, family trust, trust for estate, etc., the important thing to remember here is that the trustee(s) has control over the trust, and it is him or her who decides when to buy or redeem your mutual fund investments.

  Because trusts are legal documents typically drawn up by attorneys, each type is different and their tax consequences are as individual as the agreements are themselves. The best advice to anyone wanting to have their mutual fund shares held in a trust is to consult their tax attorney and their accountant.

Having your account registered properly is very important. Make sure all questions and concerns you have about that process are answered by either your tax accountant, your financial advisor, or a fund representative before opening your account.

Question 74
I plan on spending half the year at my home in Massachusetts and the other half in Florida. Will the fund send my monthly checks to both places?

Sure. Provided you let them know well in advance—in writing.

To get a check from your mutual fund account sent to an address other than the one on file means more often than not sending the fund family a signature-guaranteed letter. Once that's received, the check can be sent anywhere.

One reminder: Make sure all the people whose names are registered on your fund account travel with you. Why? Because most fund families require signatures from everyone listed on the account for their checks to be cashed.

Question 75
When I die, will my mutual fund account be subject to probate?

The answer to that question all depends upon the amount of money in your estate, the type of account you've opened, how it is registered, and the probate laws in the state you call home.

Probate is a state process that's used to value the assets of the deceased person, determine who the creditors are, pay the creditors, and distribute the remaining assets to the beneficiaries. Deciding what is subject to probate and what's not varies from state to state. As a rule of thumb, my resources tell me that any of the assets you own individually, like those in a mutual fund account, will more than likely be subject to probate. But because each case is different, consult a tax attorney. He or she can address the question as it relates to your individual situation.

Question 76
I'd like to open an account
for my 3-year-old daughter.
How can I do that?

Very easily.

Opening an account for a minor means having the mutual fund account registered as either a Uniform Gift to Minor Act (UGMA) account or a Uniform Transfer to Minor Act (UTMA).

Both are similar in that both are ways of registering custodial accounts for minors. They differ in the kinds of assets that can be placed in each and in age restrictions and availability. For example, in Florida, the age of majority is 21. In Connecticut, it's 18. See your broker or financial advisor for the particulars.

Question 77
What's the "Kiddie Tax"?

That's the name for the tax levied on accounts opened for minors.

Uncle Sam doesn't let anyone escape tax consequences. So, if you've opened a fund account for a minor via either a UGMA or UTMA account, even though the account owner is a minor, there are still taxes from the investment that need to be paid. Who pays the tax all depends upon who wants to write the check—mom, dad, the minor, grandma, or whoever.

The "Kiddie Tax" applies to anyone aged 14 and under. In general, it works like this:

- The first $650 of investment income or other unearned income is exempt from federal income tax.
- The next $650 is taxed at the child's rate, normally 15 percent.
- Investment income exceeding $1,300 is taxed at the parent's rate.

After age 14, income is taxed at the child's own rate. And that's how the rules read in 1997. Of course, all of that is subject to change, so make sure to consult your advisor for the particulars.

Question 78
I work outside of the country where use of joint-tenancy-in-common is not an option because males cannot leave money to wives or daughters in their probated estates. A designation of beneficiary (DOB) skirts probate. Where can I find a list of fund families that offer designations of beneficiaries?

While there are no lists around naming the fund families that carry DOBs, not to worry. According to industry pros at AIM Funds, the space for a DOB is only found on retirement account application forms. So, they ought to be a part of every fund family's retirement account application forms. They are a part of those forms because IRS regulations specify that the named beneficiary supersedes everything, including what might be in your will.

But it sounds as though the bigger question here might be a how-can-I-transfer-my-account-holdings-upon-my-death one. If that's the case, you'll need to know about a Transfer On Death (TOD) form.

A Transfer on Death (TOD), adopted under the Uniform Transfer on Death Security Registration Act, allows its owner to do a couple of things: The first is to maintain all control over when fund shares are bought, redeemed, or transferred; the second, to arrange a non-probate transfer of the fund's assets to a named beneficiary.

TODs aren't available in all types of registrations. Only accounts held in a single name, joint tenants with rights of survivorship, and tenants by the entirety can use them. They also can't be registered in all states. Currently, about 35 of the 50 states allow TOD. That means you can check with your fund family to find out if TODs are allowable in your home state. If so, you can request a form from them and make the appropriate changes to your account.

Question 79
What is the capital gains tax? And why and when do I have to pay it?

Ah...taxes. Wouldn't it be great if we didn't have to pay 'em? But they are a fact of life in the investing world whether we like it or not.

A capital gains tax is a tax that's levied any time a security is sold at a higher price than it was purchased at. We pay a capital gains tax because it's a part of the tax law. And, while you can incur a capital gains tax liability at any time during the year, those tax consequences are to be recorded in the year that they were received. So any capital gains consequences that have come your way in 1998 will be paid in 1999, when you file and pay the IRS your 1998 taxes.

In the mutual fund arena, expect to be levied a capital gains tax when you liquidate, i.e., redeem, shares of your fund, and when the fund makes its capital gains distributions. By law, all mutual funds must pass on any dividend and interest income and capital gains to their shareholders. That's the reason why mutual fund shareholders usually find themselves with a capital gains tax that needs to be paid each year. The exception here is if your fund shares are held in a tax-deferred account such as an IRA. Taxes on those accounts are paid at a later date.

Question 80
How do I know if I've incurred a long-term or short-term capital gain on my fund investments?

That will depend upon the length of time that you've held the fund shares before liquidating them. And that length of time is ever-changing.

With tax laws changing all the time, it's really easy for the average investor to be confused. Fortunately, mutual fund families know this, and most have either excellent tax related brochures and booklets that they offer their shareholders or a staff of tax experts willing to help with their tax concerns.

According to a Vanguard Group brochure about understanding the Tax Relief Act of 1997, "The new tax law makes income taxation significantly more complex because there are now not two, but three possible holding periods for most investments, with three corresponding sets of capital gains rates."

Here's a look at what those various capital gains tax rates are:

- *Short-term: 12 months or less.* Own your fund investments for a period of 12 months or less and the gains will be taxed at ordinary income rates, the top rate being 39.6 percent.
- *Mid-term: From 12 months through 18 months.* This new holding period has a taxable top rate of 28 percent.
- *Long-term. More than 18 months.* The top taxable rate here is 20 percent.

There's also a "super" long-term capital gains rate that Vanguard says "will generally apply only for assets bought after the year 2000 and held more than five years, i.e., sold after the year 2005." The taxable rate on transactions falling into this category will range from 8 percent to 18 percent.

As always, it's best to consult a tax advisor for the real skinny on the tax consequences resulting from your mutual fund investments.

Question 81
Now that I've made a few investments in mutual funds, I understand that the paperwork when selling them is daunting. Any truth to that?

Well... You've definitely got to have your ducks in a row if you'd like to make your what-happens-when-I-sell-my-funds paperwork a breeze.

That means keeping fund records and having them in order. The best way to do that is to create a filing system—which could be something as simple as a big envelope, a manila folder, or whatever—for every single mutual fund account that you own. So, if you are a shareholder in five different mutual funds, have five separate files—one for each.

In that file keep all the statements the fund sends you. And most importantly, keep every single year-end account statement. A simple system like this, I guarantee, will save you time later on when you decide to liquidate fund shares.

As to calculating taxes, because I'm not a tax expert I'll use the American Century 1997 Mutual Fund Tax Guide as my reference source. I realize that by the time this book is published, American Century will have a new 1998 tax guide out (get it free by calling 1-800-345-2021), and that there will no doubt be changes in the tax laws, so use the information below as a guideline to learn about the various ways taxes can be calculated on mutual funds and not as gospel.

Here's some of what's in that brochure.

Determining Your Cost Basis
Taxable capital gains and losses occur when fund shares

are redeemed. This includes any of the following transactions:
- redeeming your fund shares
- exchanging shares between funds

Note: Cost basis is not applicable for shares transferred within the same fund from another account with different ownership.

To calculate your cost basis, you must first determine the purchase price for all of the shares you own in a particular fund. Over time, you may have purchased shares at different prices and in differing amounts. In addition, any reinvested distributions are considered purchases and must be included in your calculations.

You may use your annual account statements to identify every purchase you made for a particular account. Once you have determined the purchase price for the different shares you own, you can calculate your cost basis using one of the three methods allowed by the IRS.

The Three Methods of Calculating Cost Basis
The IRS currently allows you to calculate your mutual fund cost basis using any one of the following three methods:

- Average Cost (Single Category or Double Category) Method
- FIFO (First-In, First-Out) Method
- Specific Identification Method

Each method has advantages and disadvantages, depending on your tax situation. Your tax advisor can help you decide which method best suits your needs.

Before you choose your method, keep this in mind: your cost basis must reflect the price of all of your purchases, including any reinvested dividend and capital gain distributions. Over time, reinvested distributions can account for a substantial portion of your purchases; by omitting these transactions from your cost basis, you will report a larger capital gain or smaller capital loss than you actually have. Also, once a method is chosen for a particular fund, you cannot change your method unless you have approval to change in writing from the IRS.

To illustrate the three methods for calculating cost basis, let's use the account activity in XYZ Fund, listed in the chart.

XYZ Fund

Date of Transaction	Trans-action	Dollar Amount	Price per Share	Number of Shares	Share Balance
11/02/94	Purch-by Check	$7,700	$11.00	700	700
11/30/94	Reinv-Dividend	$240	$12.00	20	720
01/30/95	Purch-by exchange from acct #00000	$9,000	$10,00	900	1,620
06/27/95	Purch-by Check	$5,600	$14.00	400	2,020
Total Invested		**$22,540**			**2,020 Shares**

Based on this hypothetical example, we will calculate a cost basis using each of the three methods, assuming a December 1, 1997 redemption of 100 shares at $13 per share (proceeds totaled $1,300).

The Average Cost Methods

Both average cost methods (single category and double category) have special requirements that you should carefully consider:

• To use either single category or double category, you must state on your tax return, or on an attachment to your tax return, which method you've chosen.
• If you choose either of the average cost methods, the IRS requires you to use that method for all accounts registered with your taxpayer identification number in that particular mutual fund. However, you may use different methods for other mutual funds. For example, if you used the average cost method (single method) for an XYZ fund account, you must use this method for all of your XYZ accounts. You may use a different method for your other funds.
• Once you have chosen to use average cost method, you cannot change methods for any accounts in that particular fund without requesting and receiving permission

from the IRS.
- Average cost may be used only for mutual funds. It cannot be used for any other investments, including individual stocks and bonds.

Single Category Method

The single category method allows you to average the cost of all of your shares, regardless of the amount of time you've held them.

Example:

For your XYZ Fund account, your total cost, including reinvested dividends, was $22,540, and you owned 2,020 shares total. Your average cost is $22,540 divided by 2,020, or $11.16 per share. Your resulting cost basis for 100 redeemed shares is $11.16 x 100, or $1,116.

On your tax return, you need to declare what your holding period was.

In this example, your sale of 100 shares resulted in a long-term capital gain of $184 ($1,300 − $1,116 = $184) which is generally subject to a tax at a maximum rate of 20 percent.

When using this method, it is important to note that the cost basis for the remaining shares in your account is now equal to the average cost you calculated. In the above example, 1,920 shares remain in the account after the sale; the purchase price of all 1,920 shares is now $11.16 (the average cost), regardless of the original purchase price. If additional shares are purchased in the future, your average cost will change. For example, if you purchase 500 additional shares at $12.00 per share, your new average cost would be $11.33 per share ($27,424 divided by 2,420).

Double Category Method

The double category method requires you to calculate two average cost bases—a short-term cost basis for shares bought less than a year ago and a long-term cost basis for shares bought a year ago or more. (Note: To date no changes have been made by the IRS to calculate a separate basis for shares held longer than 18 months.) Despite the extra work, some investors prefer this method because it allows them to choose whether their gains and losses are short- or long-term.

Example:

In your XYZ Fund account, you have held 720 shares—your 700 original shares plus 20 shares bought by reinvested dividends on November 30, 1996—for more than a year. When you divide $7,940 (the total cost of the shares) by 720 (the total number of shares), you get an average long-term share cost of $11.03.

In addition, you have held 1,300 shares—900 shares purchased on January 8, 1997, and 400 shares purchased on June 27, 1997—for less than a year. When you divide $14,600 (the total cost of the shares) by 1,300 (the total number of shares), you get an average short-term share cost of $11.23.

If you redeem 100 long-term shares on December 1, 1997, your cost basis would be $1,103, and a long-term capital gains of $197 would result ($1,300 – $1,103 = $197). In addition, because the shares sold have been held for greater than 18 months, your short-term capital gain would have been $177 ($1,300 – $1,123 = $177).

Note: You must specify to the fund company the category from which the shares are to be redeemed or exchanged. Unless the fund confirms your specification in writing, you must first charge the shares sold against the long-term category, oldest shares first, and then any remaining shares sold against the short-term category.

The FIFO Method

Using the First-In, First-Out (FIFO) Method you assume that the first shares you redeem are the first ones you bought. If you don't specify another method, the IRS will assume that you have used FIFO.

Example:

Applying FIFO to your account in XYZ Fund, you are selling 100 of the 700 original shares you bought on May 2, 1996. Your cost basis for those 100 shares is 100 multiplied by the $11 purchase price, for a total of $1,100.

Because you held the shares for more than one year, you would have realized long-term capital gains of $200 ($1,300 – $1,100 = $200).

The Specific Identification Method

This method allows you to choose which shares are redeemed, as long as you identify the shares at the time of the redemption. For each redemption or exchange, you must request written confirmation from the fund identifying which shares were redeemed. The confirmation should specify the number of shares redeemed, the date the shares were purchased, and the purchase price of the shares.

While this method allows you to minimize or maximize gains and losses, it also requires you to keep written records confirming which shares were redeemed. You should keep a copy of all confirmation letters; the IRS may request them. Your tax advisor can give you more information about record-keeping requirements.

Example:

In XYZ Fund, using specific identification, you will have a short-term capital loss if you redeem 100 of the shares you purchased in June 1997. Your cost basis for those 100 shares is 100 multiplied by the $14 purchase price, for a total of $1,400. In this hypothetical example, your redemptions of 100 shares resulted in a short-term capital loss of $100 ($1,300 – $1,400 = –$100) because you held the shares for less than one year.

Got that? If not, don't hesitate to consult your fund family for questions you have about the tax consequences of your investment. Or see your CPA or accountant.

Question 82
What kinds of forms will my mutual fund send me so that I'll be able to complete my taxes?

By the end of January each year, expect to receive the following forms from your fund family regarding activity in your account for the previous year:

- *An annual statement.* On this form you'll find a listing of all the activity that's occurred in your account during the calendar year. Everything from fund share purchases to redemptions to fund distributions will be on this form. Because this is an important form, make sure to keep it and collect them for every year that you are a shareholder in the fund.
- *Form 1099-B.* On this form you'll find any withdrawal transactions (redemptions or exchanges) that you've had from your fund account(s) during the year. You'll need this information to complete Schedule D of your federal tax return. And don't forget, the information on Form 1099-B is reported to both you and the IRS.
- *Form 1099-DIV.* This form will show you the taxable ordinary income and capital gains that have been distributed to your account(s) during the year. Information on Form-1099-DIV is also reported to both you and the IRS.

Question 83
I've heard that I can get out of paying a fund's capital gains tax. Is that true?

Although mutual funds—by law—must pass on any capital gain, dividend, and interest income to their shareholders, if you play your cards right and put some thought into the timing of your initial mutual fund investment, you can avoid facing any capital gains consequence that it might kick off. But this will probably be a one-time event and happen in the calendar year in which you first invest in the fund. Every year thereafter, as a fund shareholder, if the fund makes a capital gains distribution, you'll have those taxes to report and pay. Unless of course the fund investment is held in a qualified retirement account or you're a short-term fund investor who sells your shares each year before the capital gains distribution record date.

To avoid getting hit with this tax right out of the box, plan ahead and put off investing in a fund until after it has made its capital gains distribution. Since most funds typically declare income dividends and capital gains distributions in December, putting off buying those fund shares until after the fund's record date could save you some money come April 15th.

To find out when a fund's record date is—the date it plans on making its distributions—and how much those distributions are likely to be, simply call the fund's 800 number and ask. Or, contact your financial advisor. He or she will be able to help you, too.

Question 84
How easy is it to open an
on-line account?

It's real easy to open the account—that only takes a few minutes. But, don't expect to do any business right away. My experience shows that opening an account is one thing, but buying any securities on-line couldn't happen until I had a stash of money in my account.

How much money you'll need in your account before you can make an investment will depend upon the guidelines of the firm with which you're doing business. So, if on-line brokerage accounts is the way you want to go when investing in mutual funds, it's imperative to *plan ahead*.

Question 85
I'd like to buy my mutual funds on-line. Is there a list of brokerage firms that do business on the Web?

In early September 1998, *The Wall Street Journal* looked at the services that the largest on-line brokers offered. Below are the names, Web site addresses, and types of investments you can purchase through them. The firms are listed in alphabetical order in the table below.

Firm	Web Address	Investments
Ameritrade	www.ameritrade.com	Stocks, mutual funds, options
Charles Schwab	www.schwab.com	Stocks, corporate and U.S. Treasury's, mutual funds, options
Datek Online	www.datek.com	Stocks and mutual funds
DLJdirect	www.dljdirect.com	Stocks, U.S. Treasury's, mutual funds, options
Discover Brokerage Direct	www.dbdirect.com	Stocks, U.S. Treasury's, mutual funds, options
Dreyfus Brokerage Services	www.edreyfus.com	Stocks, mutual funds, options
E*Trade	www.etrade.com	Stocks, U.S. Treasury's, municipal, corporate, and agency bonds, mutual funds, options

Firm	Web Address	Investments
Fidelity Investments	www.fidelity.com	Stocks, U.S. Treasury's, municipal bonds, mutual funds, options
National Discount Brokers	www.ndb.com	Stocks, mutual funds
Quick & Reilly	www.quick-reilly.com	Stocks, U.S. Treasury's, mutual funds, options
Suretrade	www.suretrade.com	Stocks, U.S. Treasury's, mutual funds, options
Waterhouse Investor Services	www.waterhouse.com	Stocks, mutual funds, options

Source: *The Wall Street Journal*, September 8, 1998

Question 86
Have fund families' Web sites changed much over the years?

Plenty.

A few years ago, a mutual fund family's home page looked a lot like print ad—heavy on sales pitches and light on content. Now, much of that has changed: On-line fund families today offer their readers ways to open accounts, receive prospectuses, and review fund performances, plus offer a bevy of educational information, too.

Take a look at Vanguard's Web site, for instance, and you can do things like test your mutual fund knowledge and learn about investing for retirement. Look at their Investor Education site via The Vanguard Online University and you'll find information on subjects including the basics of mutual fund investing, what the differences are between saving and investing, and how to build a balanced portfolio.

The Calvert Group's home page will tune you in to everything from understanding what socially responsible investing is all about to understanding risk and understanding the securities markets. The first few paragraphs under their Understanding Investments, for instance, talks about how the world influences investments. It reads like this: "Before getting into the meat and potatoes of individual investments, it's important to understand the impact certain events can have on all investments.

"No investment opportunity, no matter how promising or

strong, is immune to the forces of the economy. Financial markets and the economy are like the ecosystem—all elements are interdependent, and changes that occur in one area can affect other areas, either directly or indirectly." These are definitely words fund investors need to remember. Calvert's site has a section titled, *Do You Know What You Own?* To find out whether a fund—any fund—owns tobacco stocks, all you have to do is enter the fund's name in the appropriate space, hit "go" and in about a minute you'll find out that fund's tobacco holdings, the holdings' market value, and what other companies are in the fund's portfolio. I entered the name "Magellan" and found out that as of 3/31/97 it owned Philip Morris, RJR Nabisco, Imperial Tobacco, and Group PLC. At Muhlenkamp's site, there's even an educational slide show. At Founders Investor site, there is information for individual investors, institutional investors, and financial advisors. In short, most fund families have done a great job of making their Web sites attractive, informative, and educational.

But as nifty and informative as a fund's Web site pages can be, weeding through the couple of hundred mutual fund sites and looking for the good ones is time consuming. To hasten that task, McGladrey & Pullen, a nationally certified public accounting and consulting firm, browsed existing mutual fund Web sites in June 1997, then judged each based upon five criteria: their information, function, design, quality, and connectivity.

Winners in each of those categories were Founders, for information; Fidelity, for function; Crabbe Huson for design; American Century for quality; and Vanguard for connectivity.

The top twenty fund Web pages that were rated the highest by McGladrey & Pullen, in alphabetical order, are:

www.americancentury.com
www.calvertgroup.com
www.fidelity.com
www.founders.com
www.gabelli.com

www.invesco.com
www.janusfunds.com
www.jhancock.com
www.kemper.com
www.leggmason.com
www.lindnerfunds.com
www.mfs.com
www.oppenheimerfunds.com
www.putnaminv.com
www.schwab.com
www.scudder.com
www.steinroe.com
www.strong-funds.com
www.troweprice.com
www.vanguard.com

Web Marketing Associates, a Boston-based Web site review firm, also looks at fund Web sites. They gave their Best of Industry Award to Stein Roe's Web site in 1998. The three fund families receiving their Standard of Excellence Award from them that year were the Calvert Group, the Winthrop Funds, and INVESCO.

Consider, however, all of this old news, and only a starting point for information. Why? Because fund Web sites are changing almost daily. And as they do, they're becoming better and better.

Question 87
You've written about popular mutual fund Web sites. But what about other, perhaps less self-serving sites, ones that carry information about mutual funds on them. Are there any like that?

Yes, there are a number of good sources for mutual fund information on-line. Some, like The Street (www.thestreet.com), have a subscription rate that's got to be paid in order to get at their mutual fund information once your free viewing period has ended. But paying isn't always necessary, as there are a handful of excellent free sites worth your visit. And the number of them increases almost daily.

While it's impossible to provide all of the names and Web addresses of sites providing fund data, following are just a few of them. Sites named are free and listed in alphabetical order:

- *Fund Alarm* (www.fundalarm.com). This is a mutual fund information site with an attitude that contains data on over two thousand mutual funds. Visit it and you'll fund plenty of tabloid-type commentary, plus fund news and an interesting section on changes in mutual fund portfolio managers.

  Fund Alarm also has a 3-ALARM system that points out laggard funds, meaning those that have underperformed their benchmarks for the past 12-month, three-year, and five-year periods. "For those who like viewing train wrecks," the site reads, "Each month we post a table of only 3-ALARM funds."

On Feb. 4, 1998, when I visited this site, there were 27 funds listed on the brink of meeting FundAlarm's criteria for under-performing their benchmarks. When I visited again on September 20, 1998, there were too many to count. FundAlarm needs to be read with an open mind and 3-ALARM listed funds are not automatically assumed to be bad investments.

- *Investor Guide* (www.investorguide.com). The mutual fund pages here provide an incredible source of fund news and data from the industry's most recognized companies. You can research Morningstar data, or the performance data from CNNfn, Lipper Analytical Services, and *Forbes* magazine. Or read *The Wall Street Journal*'s fund performance reports, review *Kiplinger's* Top Funds, and scan *Worth* magazine and *Money* magazine's annual mutual fund guides. There's also a section on closed-end funds.

- *Morningstar* (www.morningstar.net). From the brand name that helped make "mutual funds" household words, a stop or two here might find you canceling your hard copy subscription to use only their on-line service. Why? Because, depending upon your needs, there is plenty of fund information available free at www.morningstar.com.

Along with fund performance numbers, readers can also screen funds and come up with a list of them that meet their investing criteria based upon a fund's past performance. It's also got all the bells and whistles you might expect, plus commentary from Russ Kinnel, their Morningstar Fund Spy.

- *Mutual Funds Interactive* (www.brill.com or www.mutualfundsinteractive.com) has been around for years and has established itself as "The Web's #1 Mutual Fund Resource." While you can find daily news, weather, sports, and market reports at this site, you can also read fund columns from a handful of nationally recognized mutual fund columnists, including James L. Tyson, Gail Liberman, and me.

You can also search their business-only book lists and order books at a discount, review newsletters, learn about investing in mutual funds, and much, much more. If you're looking for a good starting point for fund information, Mutual Funds Interactive is a great place to begin. Three other popular mutual fund sites are

- *Smart Money* (www.dowjones.com/smart/)
- *Quicken* (www.quicken.com/investments/mutualfunds/)
- *Yahoo* (www.yahoo.com)

Like the others mentioned, they too offer readers valuable fund insights and resources, all for free and at their fingertips.

Part 6
Odds and Ends

Everybody has a drawer, shoebox, or something at home or at the office that's just full of stuff. Stuff that's too precious to throw away but doesn't really fit with anything else. That's what Part 6 is all about. Want to know how much money is invested in funds, or find out how a fund spends its money, or what the largest fund families are? You'll find those answers among the many Q&As covered in the following pages.

Question 88
How much money is in
mutual funds, anyway?

Plenty. According to the Investment Company
Institute (ICI), the trade association for the fund
industry that keeps tabs on about 95 percent of all
funds out there, at the end of July 1998 there was
$5.158 trillion dollars in mutual funds.

The breakdown of fund type to assets held is as follows:

Type of fund	Assets, in billions of dollars, at the end of July 1998
Stock funds	$2,814.1
Hybrid funds	356.3
Taxable bond funds	508.7
Municipal bond funds	283.2
Taxable money market funds	1,015.6
Tax-free money market funds	180.5
Total	**$5,158.4**

Question 89
What percentage of total mutual fund assets are in stock funds?

According to the Investment Company Institute, the trade association for the mutual fund industry, at the end of June 1998 stock mutual funds accounted for $2.841 trillion, or slightly over 55 percent, of total mutual fund industry assets. The other 45 percent was invested in bond funds, hybrid funds, and money market funds as follows: Bond funds had assets of $784.32 billion, or more than 15 percent, of total industry assets; hybrid funds had assets of $357.28 billion, or nearly 9 percent, of total industry assets; and money market funds had assets of $1.169 trillion, or almost 23 percent, of total industry assets.

**Question 90
Who owns more shares
of stock—mutual fund
companies or individual
investors?**

I bet you'll be surprised by this answer because it's not mutual funds. The individual investor owns more shares of stock.

In 1998, numbers from the 1997 *Security Industry Fact Book* show that 47 percent of all stocks were held by individuals, 23 percent by pension funds, 14 percent by mutual funds, and the rest by corporations and insurance companies.

Question 91
Is there a trade association for mutual funds that anyone can tap into?

Yes, it is called The Investment Company Institute (ICI), and it is the national trade association for the mutual fund industry.

The ICI is located in Washington, D.C. It is a nonprofit organization, and its members account for approximately 95 percent of total industry assets. The number of mutual funds included in the ICI's roster currently is 6,661 open-end funds, 443 closed-end funds, and 10 sponsors of unit investment trusts.

Along with offering research and information to people like me who write about funds, the ICI also conducts studies, puts together programs, and publishes educational brochures available to the public.

Booklets the ICI offers free to the public include the following:

- "A Guide to Understanding Mutual Funds." This 32-page guide contains a variety of information, including things like the answers to questions investors need to understand about mutual funds, ideas on investment goal setting, and how-to's on developing realistic long-term investment expectations.
- "A Guide to Bond Mutual Funds." This piece addresses the basics of bond fund investing and looks at subjects such as risk and reward and yield and return.

- There is also a series of three investor guides—one about mutual funds, another on closed-end funds, and a third on unit investment trusts—that the ICI makes available. In each, the basic features of the investment are discussed along with information about fees and expenses. All three of the guides are available in English and Spanish.

To get any or all of the booklets mentioned, simply request them in writing. The ICI's address is: ICI, P.O. Box 27850, Washington, DC 20038-7850.

You can also visit the ICI's Web site for information. That address is: www.ici.org.

Question 92

I've been invested in mutual funds for 11 years and have enjoyed good success with the Janus family of funds. At this point in my career, I'd like to diversify into other fund families. Is there a source that rates entire fund families? Also, are there any fund families that you feel are well-positioned for both the near and long term?

For the past few years, a story about the top fund families in America has appeared in *Barron's* magazine. In 1998, that story was published in the February 9 issue with fund performance ratings based upon 1997 numbers provided by Lipper Analytical Services.

To be in that year's running, fund families had to meet certain criteria, one of which was offering a variety of funds with various investment objectives. So, if a fund family had at least three general equity funds, one world equity fund, one mixed equity fund, two taxable bond funds, one tax-exempt fund, and one money market fund, they were a part of the research. Bear in mind, those criteria restrictions automatically knocked out smaller fund groups. Consequently, findings from this research did not include the entire universe of open-end funds.

In the end, there were 84 funds listed in the 1998 Barron's story. Below are the names of 5 top-ranked fund families over three different time periods—one year, three years, and five years.

- The top-performing fund families in 1997 were: (1) Eaton Vance; (2) USAA; (3) Alliance Capital; (4) Fidelity; and (5) Suntrust Banks.
- The top five fund families over the last five years (1992 thru 1997) were: (1) the Oppenheimer Funds; (2) Vanguard; (3) the American Funds; (4) Fidelity; and (5) Miller Anderson & Sherrerd.
- Over the last 10 years (1987 thru 1997) they were: (1) Vanguard; (2) Smith Barney; (3) Oppenheimer Funds; (4) Fidelity; and (5) Merrill Lynch.

In August 1998, Jay Schabacker, author of a newsletter titled *Mutual Fund Investing*, also published a list of the top fund families. Criteria used in determining his best-of-the-pack included looking at low- and no-load fund families that offered what he concluded were "safe, low-risk, low expense funds." Fourteen funds made the grade. Five fund families that made Schabacker's top rankings were: (1) Fidelity; (2) T. Rowe Price; (3) Janus; (4) Dreyfus; and (5) Vanguard.

As you can see by comparing these different listings, the criteria used in the research plays a big part in how the fund families stack up. Plus, there's more to being a good fund family than mere fund performance. Things like being able to communicate with a fund representative when you've got questions, having statements that are easy to read, and being informed about market conditions and changes in fund management and portfolio holdings also play a big part in shareholder satisfaction.

When it comes to suggesting which fund families might be "well-positioned" for the future, because no one knows what tomorrow will bring, that's tough to answer. But if I were looking for a good fund complex to work with, I'd try my best to step back and take an overall objective view looking at things like—

- the number of funds in the family;
- the number—and variety—of funds I would have an interest in investing in that family;
- the long- and short-term performance numbers on those funds;
- the kind of shareholder communications the fund family has in place, i.e., the kinds of newsletters, research, etc., that they make available to their shareholders;
- how comprehensive and reader-friendly the monthly statements, annual reports, and prospectuses are;
- how much help the fund family provides at tax time;
- whether initial investment requirements, and subsequent investing amounts, fit into my budget;
- the overall reputation of the fund family; and
- how competitive the fund's sales charges and annual expenses are industry wide.

The more discriminating you are, the happier you're likely to be with your fund family choices.

Question 93
What are the largest fund families around today?

Here's a list of the top ten:

TEN LARGEST FUND COMPLEXES
at the end of June 1998

Complex	Percent of Market	Assets (Billions)	Rank
Fidelity Investments	12.87%	$591,403.9	1
Vanguard Group	8.27%	$379,739.9	2
Capital Research	5.62%	$258,094.2	3
Merrill Lynch	4.27%	$196,357.4	4
Putnam Funds	3.91%	$179,594.9	5
Franklin Templeton	3.82%	$175,320.4	6
Morgan Stanley/DW	3.20%	$146,944.0	7
Amvescap PLC	2.51%	$115,102.1	8
Smith Barney, Inc.	2.18%	$100,023.5	9
Scudder Kemper Inv.	2.10%	$96,403.3	10

Source: Dalbar Financial Services

Question 94
What's a good way to prepare my head for flat or bear market returns on my fund investments?

 Most people born in the 1970s and beyond don't have a clue as to what an extended bear stock market looks like performance-wise, or feels like emotionally. But some of their parents and grandparents do.

Along with reading about the history of the investing markets, there's often no better source of actual fact finding and research than talking with people who have lived through time periods when their investments weren't showing the kinds of returns they'd hoped. This means that there is plenty to be learned from folks over 50 years of age.

Another good thing to do is pretend. Ask yourself questions like: Could you still cover living expenses, finance near-term goals, and live with the idea of not recovering market losses for a few years or more if your stock portfolio, currently valued at $500,000, lost 25 percent, or dropped $125,000? Or, the $10,000 you had in a fund fell in value to $7,500? Or the $2,000 to $1,500?

Really thinking about the impact of a bear market on your investments ought to help you prepare for one. So will understanding that volatility and market corrections are just part of life in the stock market.

Question 95
What's the difference between a fund's redemption/purchase fee and a front- or back-end load?

Who gets the money.

When front- and back-end load fees are paid, that money goes to the fund's management company and fund distributors. That's how brokers, for instance, get paid for their services when selling you a fund. But a redemption fee, and/or a purchase fee—which, by the way, is a fee that only a few funds charge when redeeming fund shares—doesn't go to the broker or fund family. It goes back into the fund and gets added to its net assets.

Question 96
I want to see how a fund spends its money. Where will I find that information?

A mutual fund's statement of additional information, a booklet that all fund families publish but aren't required to send out to their shareholders unless they specifically ask for it, will tell you about the operational side of the fund.

To learn all that you can about a fund, you'll have to do some collective reading and read its prospectus and its annual, semiannual, and quarterly reports. Then ask for a copy of its statement of additional information from either your broker, your financial advisor, or the fund family itself.

Question 97
If the stock market were to fall precipitously, do you think a lot of people would sell shares of their stock funds?

That's hard to try and figure out.

After the stock market crash in 1987, folks got a first-hand glimpse of how quickly stock prices can fall and then climb back up again. Whether that experience will mean investors hold on to their stocks in coming market corrections is difficult to estimate, but studies show that they are likely to.

The Investment Company Institute (ICI), for one, has survey data indicating that stock fund shareholders are typically experienced investors with a long-term orientation. According to an ICI study covering the years 1945-95, stock fund shareholders did not sell their fund shares in large numbers during various times when the stock market fell. The report showed that the largest outflow of money within that frame happened during and immediately after the 1987 stock market crash. The amount of assets moving out of stock funds then only amounted to 4.5 percent of the total assets in stock funds. After the downturn of stocks on October 27, 1997, net outflows from stock funds were hardly noticeable. But, when the market has experienced long periods of down and flat markets, things were different. For instance, most stock funds experienced outflows of cash during the 11 years beginning with 1971 and ending in 1982 when the stock market was anything but robust. At that time, it was money market funds that were gathering assets and enjoying a heyday.

What will typically determine people's moves under extreme—and not so extreme—market conditions is investor sentiment. And investors are notorious for getting out of the market just as it hits its peaks—both its high and low ones. All of which means, forget the numbers, the prospects, and the promises; it's our moods that seem to matter the most on Wall Street. Knowing that could save and make you some money.

Question 98
To whom do I complain if I don't think I've gotten a fair deal with my mutual fund investment?

If by a "fair deal" you mean that you feel that your broker or the firm he or she represents didn't disclose enough information about the fund(s) they recommended, or you believe they misled you in any fashion, you can contact the National Association of Securities Dealers (NASD). They have district offices around the country. For more information, call them at the NASD Public Disclosure Phone Center at 1-800/289-9999. Or visit their Web site at: www.nasd.com.

Here's a listing of the NASD Regional Offices along with their phone numbers:

Atlanta, GA	404/239-6100
Denver, CO	303/446-3100
New York, NY	212/858-4000
Chicago, IL	312/899-4400
Kansas City, MO	816/421-5700
Philadelphia, PA	215/665-1180
Cleveland, OH	216/694-4545
Los Angeles, CA	213/627-2122
San Francisco, CA	415/882-1200
Dallas, TX	972/701-8554
New Orleans, LA	504/522-6527
Seattle, WA	206/624-0790

As for other complaints, you can contact the Securities

and Exchange Commission (SEC) at The Office of Consumer Affairs, 450 5th Street NW, Washington, DC 20549.

But before you do either, why not talk with your broker, financial representative, or fund family first and try to get the issue resolved with him or her? If that's not possible, ask for management's help. If you're still not satisfied, contact the industry watchdogs, i.e., the NASD or SEC.

Question 99
What confuses me is, how can a fund company advertise on TV that it's the #1 highest yielding fund, and yet when I check the rankings, I never see the fund mentioned?

When it comes to advertising a fund's rating or ranking, you've got to consider, among other things, that there are many, many, many different ways to rank and rate funds: by size, by category, by load (low or no-load status), by performance over the past week, month, quarter, year, etc., etc., etc. And, that almost every rating and ranking company, publication, and TV and radio financial news program has its own set of criteria for selecting top-performing funds. So someone's No. 1-ranked Lipper fund over the past 52 weeks might not ever show up on Morningstar's rating list.

As far as TV ads go, fund families usually buy their ads for commercials in blocks that cover a specific number of weeks. And unless a fund company makes it clear that the fund's performance is based on a certain time period and from a given rating or ranking company, things can get pretty confusing. Plus, outdated performance numbers can look fresh. Just as in print ads, it's the small stuff that's hard to read that can matter the most.

In the end, remember that top-performing funds change all the time, so don't just follow the ad's lead, do your own homework.

Question 100
What does it mean when a fund doesn't have one portfolio manager but is multi-managed ?

There are a host of ways to manage a mutual fund. Some fund families do it all internally. Others outsource, hiring the best and brightest portfolio managers in their respective asset classes. Some funds have teams of managers. Others rely on only one person. Today, one of the newest trends in fund management is the multi-managers. That's where different portfolio managers, from different fund families, get together to manage money—each in the style that they've built their reputations on—for one mutual fund.

The New England Star Advisers Fund was the first to introduce that concept back in 1994. Their thinking was to round up the top portfolio managers in the business and get them working together managing a portion of money in the same fund. They figured the results ought to be pretty good.

At the end of May 1998, the advisors who managed the assets for the New England Star Advisers Fund were Oakmark's Robert Sanborn, a value manager; Founder's Edward Keely, a growth manager; growth stock picker Warren Lambert, from Janus; and Jeffery Petheric and Mary Champagne, both small-cap value stock pickers from Loomis, Sayles & Company. With $1.1 billion in assets, and an average annual total return of over 23 percent at that time, the concept proved to be working. As a result, the New England funds have added two other funds to their multi-managed Star line-up: the Star Worldwide Fund and the Star Small-Cap Fund.

In 1996, SunAmerica also introduced a multi-managed series of funds. Fund managers here are asked to run their portion of the fund the same as they do in their publicly offered mutual funds.

In their Mid-Cap Growth Portfolio fund, for example, assets are divvied up equally between portfolio managers at MAS (Miller Anderson, & Sherrerd, LLP), Wellington, and T. Rowe Price.

In both SunAmerica's Style and the New England's Star funds, investors can look at the track records and investing styles of their fund managers and get a level of diversification not always available in a one-manager-one-style portfolio. If you like the idea, keep in mind that one obvious problem with multi-managed funds like these is that their annual expenses are higher. And that will affect the fund's overall performance numbers.

Question 101
Which mutual funds ought
I invest in?

Guess what? That's the third most asked question I get as a columnist. And the answer is, the ones that you like.

If you don't know what you like, let me help by pointing out that most people really want to be invested in stock funds when the market is rising, money market mutual funds when it's not, and bond funds sometimes. Beyond that, picking which precise fund, or fund family, or fund style is a question that only you can answer for yourself.

For clues on the funds that you might like to invest in, look inside yourself. If it's money you want to be accumulating, you need to sit down and think about the various ways there are to do that. Then ferret out the ones in which you would like to participate.

If it's investing in mutual funds, remember that you need to cover your bases and invest in both stock and fixed-income products. A stock fund investment without a complementary fixed-income component is like leaving your back door open during a wind storm—who knows what havoc could happen to your nest egg when there's a storm on Wall Street? Nobody. So to protect your assets, you need some funds that will provide a steady return and others with growth potential.

One of the simple truths about mutual fund investing is

that you are responsible for your money. Sure you might find someone who will tell you exactly which funds to buy, how much to put in each, and even that you'll have wonderful results from their plan. But if that plan goes amuck, the person who is ultimately responsible for how it worked is you. So, take the time to do some thoughtful thinking about your fund choices and why you've made them. Then look to see how diversified those fund choices are. Diversification might not provide you with the highest market return, but it can minimize the blows in turbulent market times.

Investing in mutual funds also requires being open to an ongoing education. Over time you'll see how various markets affect your fund choices, how different funds react in them, and how your tolerance for risk taking can change. All of those experiences can serve to make you a better investor. And one that can be handsomely rewarded over the long run. Good luck.

Glossary

Advisor An individual or organization that's employed by a mutual fund to give professional advice on the management and management practices of the funds' investments and assets.

Aggressive Growth Fund Typically one that seeks maximum capital gains as its investment objective. Current income is not a significant factor. Aggressive funds may invest in stocks of businesses ranging from micro-cap ones to fledgling companies, to new industries, or companies that have fallen on hard times, industries temporarily out of favor, emerging markets, and whatever. This type of fund is for those who are comfortable taking risks with their investment dollars.

Annualized Rate of Return The one-year return of something based on its compounded total return. For example, the seven-day returns you see on money market funds show an annualized rate of return. They are arrived at by taking the compounded effect over seven days and multiplying it by 52.

Assets Anything owned that is considered to have value. The assets of a mutual fund are made up of various securities such as stocks, bonds, and cash.

Automatic Reinvestment An investment choice for mutual fund shareholders in which the proceeds from either the fund's dividends or capital gains, or both, are automatically used to buy more shares of the fund.

Back-End Load A kind of sales charge incurred when investors redeem (or sell) shares of a fund.

Balanced Fund A type of mutual fund that generally has three investment objectives: (1) to conserve the investors' initial principal, (2) to pay current income, and (3) to promote long-term growth of both principal and income. Typically the portfolio mix of balanced funds includes bonds, preferred stocks, and common stocks.

Beta A numerical measure that indicates a fund's volatility. Following the beta formula, a fund with a beta of 1 will fluctuate in value as the market does. Funds with betas lower than 1 will be less volatile than the market. Those with betas higher than 1 will be more volatile than the market.

Bond One of the many kinds of securities, considered debt instruments. Bonds have maturity dates scheduled some time in the future, are typically issued by municipalities, corporations, and governments, and usually pay interest twice a year.

Broker/Dealer A firm that buys and sells mutual fund shares and other securities to the public.

Capital Gain A selling price that is higher than an asset's original purchase price.

Capital Gains Distributions Payments made to mutual fund shareholders that come from profits realized from the sale of the various securities within a mutual fund's portfolio. Typically these distributions are paid once a year at or near the end of the year.

Certificate of Deposit (CD) A debt instrument issued by a bank that typically pays interest to its owner.

Closed-End Investment Companies Also referred to as closed-end funds or publicly traded funds, these mutual funds issue only a fixed number of shares and are not required to create or redeem shares upon the demand of their shareholders as open-end mutual funds do. Like stocks, closed-end funds trade on the major exchanges.

Contingent Deferred Sales Load (CDSL) A kind of sales fee imposed when shares of a fund are being redeemed, or bought back, by the fund. CDSLs decline (usually by 1 percent per year) over time and therefore are sometimes called the disappearing sales charge.

Corporate Bond Fund A mutual fund designed to provide income for its shareholders as it buys interest-paying bonds of corporations, the bonds of the U.S. Treasury, or those issued by a federal agency.

Debt Investments Bonds.

Derivative One of any number of different types of financial arrangements between two parties in which their value is "derived" from the performance of some benchmark. For instance, a stock option is a common kind of derivative.

Discount With regard to closed-end funds, a term meaning that the per-share price of a closed-end fund is selling for less than the actual NAV of the securities that make up that fund's portfolio.

Discount Broker A brokerage firm whose commission rates are lower than those charged by full-service brokerage firms.

Diversification Spreading the risk. Mutual funds spread investments among a number of different securities to reduce the risk inherent in investing. Mutual fund investors diversify their fund investments by investing in a variety of different types of funds.

Dollar-Cost Averaging An investment strategy that means investing the same amount of money at regular intervals onto the same investment over time. This procedure can reduce the average per-share cost to the investor. It also allows a fund shareholder to acquire more shares when the fund's share prices are lower and fewer shares when prices are higher.

Dow Jones Industrial Average A weighted number that reflects the average of 30 actively traded blue-chip stocks.

Equity Investments Stocks.

Exchange Fee A fee some mutual funds impose upon their shareholders when they switch from one fund to another within the fund family.

Exchange Privilege An investment choice that allows mutual fund shareholders to transfer their investments from one fund to another within the same fund family. Some funds allow their shareholders to use the exchange privilege several times a year for free; others charge a fee. See also Exchange Fee.

Expenses and Management Fees Asset-based annual charges that investment companies pass on to their shareholders. These fees differ from mutual fund to mutual fund and typically range between 0.50 and 1.80 percent annually.

Expense Ratio The amount deducted from a mutual fund for operating expenses and management fees. It is expressed as a percent of the fund's average net assets.

401(k) Plan Often referred to as a salary reduction plan, a plan that gives employees the opportunity to invest pretax money into various investment plans and defer paying the taxes on that account until a later date.

Financial Markets All of the investment opportunities available in the various types of securities around the world today, including those in the stock, bond, commodity, currency, and international financial marketplaces.

Flexible Portfolio Fund A type of mutual fund in which 100 percent of the fund's assets may be invested in stocks or in bonds or in money market instruments, depending on market conditions. These funds give their money managers the greatest flexibility in anticipating or responding to economic changes.

Front-End Load A sales charge that is paid before any dollars are invested into the mutual fund of your choice.

Global Bond Fund A type of mutual fund that invests in the debt securities of companies and countries located throughout the world. Global bond funds may also invest in the United States.

Global Equity Fund A type of mutual fund that invests in securities traded throughout the world, including securities in the United States. Compared to direct investing, global funds of all types offer investors an easier avenue to investing abroad. The funds' professional money managers handle the trading and record-keeping details and deal with differences in currencies, languages, time zones, laws and regulations, and business customs and practices.

Growth and Income Fund A mutual fund that invests in the common stock of publicly held companies that have had increasing share values but also have a solid record of paying dividends. This type of fund attempts to combine long-term capital growth with a steady stream of dividend income.

Growth Fund A mutual fund that invests in the common stock of publicly held companies. The primary aim of growth funds is to produce an increase in the fund's NAV, which means that investors who buy growth funds are more interested in seeing the fund's share price rise than in receiving income from their investment.

High-Yield Bond Fund Also referred to as "junk" bond funds, these mutual funds typically have at least two-thirds of their portfolios invested in lower-rated corporate bonds, i.e., rated Baa or lower by Moody's rating service and BBB or lower by Standard & Poor's rating service. In return for the generally higher yield these bond funds offer, investors must bear a greater degree of risk.

Income Payments made to mutual fund shareholders, typically from dividends, interest, or short-term capital gains earned on a fund's portfolios of securities after deduction of operating expenses.

Income Bond Fund A type of mutual fund that seeks a high level of current income for shareholders by investing in a mix of corporate and government bonds.

Income Equity Fund A type of mutual fund that seeks a high level of current income for shareholders by investing primarily in equity securities of companies with good dividend-paying records.

Income Mixed Fund A mutual fund that seeks a high level of current income for shareholders by investing in income-producing securities that include both equity—i.e., stock—and debt—i.e., bond—instruments.

Index Fund A type of mutual fund in which the portfolios are constructed to mirror a specific market index, such as the S&P 500. Index funds are expected to provide a rate of return that will approximate or match that of the market that they are mirroring.

Individual Retirement Account (IRA) An account designed for long-term saving/investing that one may create for oneself that is subject to IRS restrictions regarding who may open the account and how much money may be invested each year.

Initial Public Offering (IPO) A corporation's first offering of its stock to the public.

International Fund A mutual fund that invests its assets in the equity securities of companies located outside the United States. Two-thirds of their portfolios must be so invested at all times if the fund is to be categorized as an international fund.

Investment The purchase of anything that carries with it the possibility of an increase in value at some later time.

Investment Advisor See Advisor.

Investment Company A mutual fund, corporation, trust, or partnership that makes investments on behalf of individuals and institutions who share common financial goals and objectives. Investment companies hire investment advisors to purchase a variety of stocks, bonds, money market instruments, or other securities that—in their judgment—will help the fund meet its investment objectives. Some of the benefits of investing through investment companies are the professional management, liquidity, and diversification of an investment company's portfolio.

Investment Company Act of 1940 The primary watchdog

law of the mutual fund industry that is a highly detailed regulatory statute that sets the standards by which mutual funds and other investment companies must operate.

Investment Company Institute (ICI) The Washington, DC-based trade association for the mutual fund industry.

Investment Objective The reason why the mutual fund was created. Examples of a fund's investment objective might be "growth of capital" or "income." But whatever it is, you'll always find it specifically spelled out in the fund's prospectus.

Keogh Plan A tax-deferred pension plan designed for the self-employed or for employees of unincorporated businesses.

Letter of Instruction A letter that specifically outlines any changes an individual would like to make in his or her shareholder account, such as change of name or address or changes in the distribution of fund proceeds.

Load A sales charge levied by a mutual fund, the maximum being 8.5 percent of a shareholder's initial investment, which is equal to 9.3 percent of the net amount invested.

Long-Term Funds According to the Investment Company Institute, any mutual fund other than a money market mutual fund. But ask a portfolio manager or financial advisor what they consider a long-term fund to be and you'll get all sorts of answers, all relating to the amount of time they think investors ought to hold on to a specific fund investment. So, the next time you hear the expression "long-term," ask some questions like, "What do you mean by long-term?"

Lump Sum A large, often one-time investment of money.

Minimum Investment Requirements The smallest amount of dollars necessary to open an account with a mutual fund, ranging from $0 to $25,000 and more. There are literally hundreds of mutual funds whose minimum investment requirements are $1,000 or less.

Money Market Deposit Accounts (MMDAs) Bank deposit investments that are insured, if the bank is insured, and designed to provide an interest rate competitive with current money market rates. MMDAs were created in 1982 to compete with money market mutual funds.

Money Market Mutual Fund (MMMF) A type of mutual fund that invests in the short-term securities sold in the money market, in which the average maturity of the entire portfolio can be no longer than 90 days. Securities that make up an MMMF's portfolio are generally considered the safest, most stable securities available and include things like Treasury bills, certificates of deposit of large banks, and commercial paper.

Mutual Fund An investment company that pools money from its shareholders and invests that money into a variety of securities, including stocks, bonds, and money market instruments. Mutual funds represent one way of investing money into a professionally managed and diversified pool of securities that—hopefully—will provide a good return on shareholders' money. The individuals selling mutual funds must have a specific license to do so.

Net Asset Value (NAV) The bottom line of a mutual fund from a per-share point of view. A fund's NAV is the market value of all of the fund's total assets, minus its liabilities, divided by the total number of outstanding shares in the fund. A fund's NAV is calculated daily. The primary reason a fund's NAV fluctuates is due to changes in market value of the holdings in a fund's portfolio.

No-Load Fund A mutual fund without a sales charge.

Objective What the investing goal of a mutual fund is.

Offering Price The per-share price of a mutual fund that includes the fund's NAV, plus the maximum sales charge of the fund if the fund has a sales charge. For mutual funds without sales charges, the offering price is the same as that fund's NAV.

Open-End Investment Companies Often called open-end mutual funds, these investment companies are obliged by law to continually create new and redeem existing shares of their funds upon the request of their shareholders. The purchasing and redeeming of these shares can be done on any business day throughout the year.

Performance Why you invest in a mutual fund. The idea behind mutual fund investing is to hopefully see your principal investment grow over time. That growth—or lack of it as the case may be—is always referred to as the fund's performance.

Portfolio All the securities owned by an institution, mutual fund, or individual are said to be held in a portfolio.

Portfolio Manager An individual or team of individuals employed by a mutual fund to manage all the securities within the fund's portfolio.

Premium What a closed-end fund is said to be trading at when the per-share price of that fund is more than the NAV of the securities that make up that fund's portfolio.

Profile Prospectus A shortened version of a fund's prospectus.

Prospectus A booklet that must be given to all mutual fund investors that outlines the reason the mutual fund was created, who manages it, what its past performance has been, what its fees are, how to buy and redeem shares, and a host of other important information. Prospectuses were created as a result of the Securities and Exchange Act of 1933 and are administered by the Securities and Exchange Commission to tell investors all the essential facts surrounding the securities they are interested in buying.

Redeem To buy back. Redeeming your fund shares is the same as selling them.

Redemption Fee A sales charge, also referred to as a back-end load, imposed when an investor redeems—or sells back—shares of the fund.

Reinvestment A service available to mutual fund shareholders in which either a portion or all of the dividends and capital gains income they've received from their mutual fund investment are automatically used to buy new shares of the fund.

Risk The chance that investors won't see the capital they've invested grow in value.

Rollover The movement of money from a pension plan into an IRA or other tax-qualified plan. Rollover monies must be reinvested within 60 days after being received to avoid a tax penalty.

Sector Fund A mutual fund whose investments focus on one specific investment category, such as energy stocks, gold, or health care companies.

Securities Investments such as stocks, bonds, or money-market instruments.

Securities and Exchange Act of 1933 A federal law requiring, among other things, that shares of a mutual fund be registered with the Securities and Exchange Commission prior to their sale and that a fund provide potential investors with a current prospectus, and limiting the kinds of advertisements a mutual fund may use.

Securities and Exchange Commission (SEC) The federal agency that governs the securities industry.

Shareholder One who owns shares of a company, corporation, or mutual fund.

Short-Term Funds All money market mutual funds. A short-term fund can also be one in which the securities held in a fund's portfolio—which in this case would only refer to bonds—have maturity dates averaging one, two, three, or four years.

Simplified Employee Pension (SEP) A kind of pension plan for the self-employed or small company owner.

Total Return The measurement of a fund's performance that includes the income received from dividends and interest, capital gains distributions, and any unrealized capital gains or losses.

Track Record The historic performance of a mutual fund. Because the various stock and bond markets run in cycles, the longer a fund's track record, the easier it is to see how that fund has performed in up and down market cycles. A fund's track record is a reflection of its past and not an indication of its future performance.

Transfer Agent The organization employed by a mutual fund that prepares and maintains records relating to the fund accounts of shareholders. Some funds serve as their own transfer agents.

12b-1 Fee A fee charged by some funds to its shareholders to cover that fund's distribution costs, such as advertising expenses and dealer compensation costs. Named after a federal government rule, 12b-1 fees are asset-based fees that typically range between 0.25 and 1.25 percent of the total assets of the fund.

Variable Annuity An investment contract acquired through a licensed insurance company representative in which money is invested in mutual funds.

Yield The income per share that gets paid to mutual fund shareholders from the dividends and interest of a fund. Yields are expressed as a percentage of the current offering price of the fund.

Index